My Rangers

My Rangers

How I Changed Scottish Football For Ever

GRAEME SOUNESS

PENGUIN
VIKING

VIKING

UK | USA | Canada | Ireland | Australia
India | New Zealand | South Africa

Viking is part of the Penguin Random House group of companies whose addresses can be found at global.penguinrandomhouse.com

Penguin Random House UK,
One Embassy Gardens, 8 Viaduct Gardens, London SW11 7BW

penguin.co.uk

Penguin Random House UK

First published 2026
001

Set in 14.8/18pt Garamond Premier Pro
Typeset by Six Red Marbles UK, Thetford, Norfolk
Printed and bound in Great Britain by Clays Ltd, Elcograf S.p.A.

The authorized representative in the EEA is Penguin Random House Ireland, Morrison Chambers, 32 Nassau Street, Dublin D02 YH68

A CIP catalogue record for this book is available from the British Library

ISBN: 978-0-241-82009-4

For my wonderful wife, Karen

Contents

Foreword

By Sir Alex Ferguson, CBE

Graeme Souness's career as a footballer is easily defined. He captained Liverpool at the time when they were on a successful run in the European Cup, winning it three times, and he captained his country twenty-seven times. One of those games for Scotland will live in my memory for ever, against England at Hampden Park in 1985. As always, it was a fiercely played game, and I will never forget Richard Gough's goal with a header in the second half. But that is not my most vivid memory; it was another battle going on in the game – Graeme Souness against Bryan Robson, the two captains going head-to-head, winner takes all! It was a masterpiece of how two players could not hide their pride or their desire to lead their country in the field. At the end of the game, the two players stood in the centre of the pitch and hugged each other! What an amazing sight. Jock Stein – who unfortunately passed away some months later – was Scotland's manager on that day, and he was euphoric at Graeme's performance, as we all were.

I write this foreword on Graeme in admiration for a real man, who did not hold grudges – as he easily could have done at my decision to leave him out of our deciding game in the 1986 World Cup in Mexico. Graeme had lost some passes in the previous two games, against Denmark and Germany, when we'd played on extremely hot days. My dilemma was that the weather forecast for the deciding game against Uruguay was also extremely hot. I spoke to Graeme and explained why I was leaving him out, and he understood. But I made my second mistake by allowing him to decide if he wanted to go on the bench or not. As history will tell you, in a game we had to win to qualify for the knockout stages, we drew 0–0. I am 100 per cent sure that if I had been able to bring Graeme on we would have benefitted from his determination, leadership and composure. In the aftermath, and throughout the years since, when Graeme has been asked about the reason to leave him out he has always said the same thing: he wasn't fit enough – meaning he spared me the blame!

Graeme's management career hit the heights when he turned Rangers FC into a force of constant success. There followed spells at his former club Liverpool, Blackburn Rovers and Newcastle United, to name just a few, where the challenges meant his experience and leadership were paramount.

During his time as a TV analyst he was, in my opinion, the best by a mile! When he gave up that role I wasn't the only one who missed his articulate assessment of the matches every week. His latest achievement could have been his most challenging and rewarding, when he swam the English Channel on behalf of the charity DEBRA, for which he is also an excellent ambassador. Like many of his admirers, I was so inspired that I just had to support him in such a brave and generous venture.

Graeme is a real gentleman and a truly great player.

Sir Alex Ferguson, CBE

Introduction: Can I Just Say Something Here?

By Chick Young

Magnificent Bastard. Although a lot of his enemies did not bother with the adjective.

The description of the former Rangers manager is one applied by fawning fans of the club who will be forever grateful for the miracle performed by the cool dude whose Ibrox memoirs you are about to peruse.

I hadn't heard the description myself and it certainly is not the light in which I see my friend bathe, but my nephew and godson and dedicated supporter of Rangers, Craig, assures me that it is one down from a deity. My invitation – sorry, command – from Souness to do the hard work on this literary gem has elevated me in the lad's eyes to unknown heights from which, looking down, I now feel quite giddy.

Souness has hung on to my coattails – have I got that the right way round? – for all of the forty years and beyond since he swung into Glasgow and set off a nuclear explosion in the once-sleepy hamlet. In the mid-eighties, Graeme rode into town somehow mistaking it for the O.K. Corral, and over the course of five incredible years left those of us making a crust in the football press wide-eyed, drop-jawed and breathless.

At the time – or at least at the beginning of this grand adventure – I was working for the *Evening Times*, the circulation area of which was the city and the greater parts of the west of Scotland, and its clubs were my beat. There was a wonderful sense of joviality about our game back then. I was living the dream, albeit I would rather have played for any of the clubs about which I wrote. The eternal dream of every Glasgow kid. To play the beautiful game and get paid for it. Apparently, I was lacking in just one commodity. Ability.

Newspapers were particularly muscular in the influence department in those days and mattered. No internet, no social media. Just people trained in the workings of the Fourth Estate, who in the main knew what they were doing. He was just Graeme in those days, an affable chap with whom I was on friendly terms, knowing him as I did as captain of Scotland. These were the kinds of people I was paid to get to know, and it was not filed under hardship.

But in the previously slumbering spring of 1986, when

the shelf life of managers was a fair bit more enduring than it is now, Rangers sacked dear Jock Wallace who, incidentally, was some man.

And so the rumblings started. Then Graeme arrived like a hurricane. He should have had a red triangle attached. His was the kind of incoming storm that would lay trees horizontal. He had his pals in the newspaper business, and I think I was somehow adopted into that family, but I had not grasped the seriousness of the situation until later that same year, on the day we flew out to the World Cup finals in Mexico. I was on the team plane preparing for the full shift of altitude training – the players trained, the press spectated and judged – for a couple of weeks in Santa Fe, New Mexico. This was to be followed by a warm-up match in Los Angeles, and the games against Denmark, West Germany and Uruguay in Mexico itself.

On the plane across the Atlantic, Graeme, who was still the captain of Scotland but who had also now been confirmed as the new Rangers manager, came down the aisle and sat beside me. He ordered a bottle of champagne, which I reluctantly accepted. Me and willpower aren't old buddies. He then asked me for advice. Yes, I know, I cannot quite believe it either.

But this was his logic. He was a boy from Edinburgh – which is just forty miles along the road from Glasgow but might as well be on another planet – and had wandered off to London as a teenager and then to Middlesbrough and Liverpool. He was, to be frank, not totally *au fait* with my native city and its wacky ways. Three-quarters of a century into my residence on this planet, I am still not sure I get it either.

But I digress. 'You are a streetwise Glaswegian. Tell me about it,' he said. I started slowly, but that champagne stuff fairly loosens the tongue and I tried to paint a picture of what I'd learned was expected from every Rangers manager I had met, from Willie Waddell onwards. Around Graeme's neck was a small cross on a chain, and I suggested to him that a fair percentage of the club's support might not see the funny side of that. He argued that it had been given to him by his then-wife, at which point I hurriedly assured him that I hadn't the slightest issue with it, and nor would any man or woman touched with a degree of sanity. Bigotry is a cancer of a lifestyle as far as I am concerned. But he had asked me about the wider view and I had guessed that there were patrons at Ibrox who were still trapped in the quicksand of the seventeenth century. And, indeed, who sang of it.

It was then he spilled the beans about the sorts of signings he wanted to make for Glasgow Rangers and his determination to set fire to the club's traditions. He spoke gloriously about the club's future with such fervour, determination and enthusiasm that it suddenly dawned on me that I should ask if this was on the record and whether I should ditch the bubbly for a notebook.

It was and I did, hence arriving in America with the time difference on my side and enough material to fill the front page, the back page and page three of my newspaper the next day. And, who knows, a book some day . . . For a fleeting time only, I was the editor's golden boy. For me that was a brief but enjoyable tour of duty with dear old George McKechnie. Normal service between me and the newspaper's gaffer was soon resumed.

But that spark ignited something, and over the next five years Graeme Souness was far from shy in feeding me information. Indeed, by the time he left the club the BBC had noticed my frequent bylines preceded with the word 'exclusive', and your old reporter had been whisked into a new world. Graeme Souness was my leg-up in my profession. I have no doubt about that.

Not much in the entire history of our game on this little outcrop of rock in the North Atlantic compares to what he did here. Scottish football has been ordinary at times, but the combined talents of the Grimms and Rowling and Tolkien could not make his exploits and escapades and experiences up. It was and is still the greatest soap opera in sport.

Graeme is a remarkable man. I can only imagine what

he was like to play against – or, for that matter, with – in his pomp, fire flaming from the nostrils, that moustache threatening like the horns of a Spanish bull intent on having a square go with the matador. I read somewhere that his one-time Liverpool teammate Michael Robinson said of him: 'I found him a very personable, cuddly chap who was actually quite vulnerable about being a human being with emotions. To this day he still tries very hard not to be this lovely cuddly person, when he really is.'

Tell that to some of his opponents, or to those players in his deployment who failed to understand the demands and complexities of his mission to restore Glasgow Rangers to the straight and narrow.

I would not want to be on his naughty step. But he is a caring man. He is focused on whatever commands his attention at any one time. He is driven, ambitious and, in stark contrast to the proverb, would indeed be very inclined to say 'boo' to a goose, or any other creature that was foolish enough to stand in his way.

And he would concede that some of the tackles which he inflicted on opponents over the years resulted in the victims looking as if they had just undergone extreme surgery. Or had been involved in a major road traffic incident. But still, I would insist, he is a very decent man.

This tale is not about his remarkable work for various charities, of his ridiculous commitment to raising funds for DEBRA and the British Heart Foundation and other unsung causes. Nor indeed is it about everything else he has done in his more than three score and ten years on this planet, a life that has been extraordinarily well lived. He took up swimming to raise funds for victims of the evil epidermolysis bullosa – butterfly skin – and has crossed channels more times than my remote.

It's not about the collection of European Cup medals jingling like loose change in his pockets, nor his cult standing in a Liverpool team which maybe bowed only to the Beatles in the places where they worship heroes on Merseyside. Nor his midfield swagger in three World Cups for Scotland, two of them as captain.

It is about just five years in the eighties – just one-fifteenth of that lifespan that I presume has a bit to journey yet – in which Graeme took Scottish football by the scruff of the neck and shook it so hard that it woke up in the real world.

It was not my idea to create this book, but I am glad someone thought of it and I am grateful that Graeme turned to me to help write it. The reliving of life forty years ago has been a sobering and did-that-really-happen experience. I know fine well that it did.

When we were discussing this book with various people interested in its publication, one gentleman in London sat open-mouthed as I told the tale of what happened from the moment Graeme arrived at Rangers. Eventually he looked at us and said: 'This isn't a book, it's a movie!'

And so it might yet prove to be, the tale recast on film, although who they would contract to perform as the hero of this story, the good Lord only knows. Magnificent Bastards, even in Hollywood, are thin on the ground.

Souness in the eighties was a force of nature and at times in the newspaper trade we wondered if we could find type sizes big enough to scream the headlines he was making. He re-energized the old business, if the truth be told, and I used to skip into the Glasgow offices of my paper rubbing my hands in anticipation of what high jinks would be unleashed from the south side that day. He seldom let us down. The signings came and went with – in the first instance – incredulity that the captain of England *and* the Auld Enemy's goalkeeper could be wooed to Govan.

And then it went off the Richter scale with Mo Johnston. My new pal in the publishing business in London could not get his mind round the fact that just four decades ago there was a football club in this country which would not knowingly sign Roman Catholics. And neither had they fielded any black players. Maurice Johnston and Mark Walters – both signed on Souness's watch – changed all that, to such an extent that no one now really knows or can surely care about the skin colour or faith of any player who signs for Rangers.

And that is the way it should be. But it sure was not in the days before Souness stormed in.

The policy of the club was an embarrassment to the city and country, and actually made Jock Stein, whose football wisdom had done for Celtic what Graeme was about to do at Ibrox, chuckle. Jock said it openly himself: if there were two young players of equal merit and one was a Catholic and the other a Protestant, then he would sign the Protestant, knowing that Rangers would not sign the other one.

It took a lot of courage to turn around all that social history. A chemistry of three men – Graeme, Maurice and the club's owner David Murray – did the trick, and society in Scotland, never mind the Rangers support, should be eternally grateful. Graeme took the club out the dark ages and locked the door behind him. He made up his own rules and followed them when it suited him.

By the time I was snuggling into life at the BBC, and Graeme had won his penultimate championship, I asked him for an exclusive one-to-one interview – in those days these things were not woven into contracts. He agreed and a camera crew and I headed over to Ibrox that May afternoon thinking that the interview would take place in the tunnel, or maybe his office. But at his suggestion a table had been put in the centre circle. It was covered with a linen tablecloth and standing on it were a jug of orange juice and two glasses. I interviewed him there and he even insisted that the cameraman climb the main stand for elevated shots of us on the pitch. The star became the director. Maybe if they do make that movie, he could just do the whole thing himself.

This book is his testimony about what went on back then. Historians in the years to come would do well to refer to his recollections of an era when there was a feeding frenzy for any nonsense that sounded as if it even remotely approximated what was happening at Glasgow Rangers.

This book is about how it really was. It was astonishing.

Maybe Craig was right. Magnificent Bastard.

Chick Young

I

The Call

It was, I recall, mid-afternoon. I was relaxing in the Italian sun . . .

In 1984 I had signed a three-year contract with Sampdoria and the lifestyle and football here suited me. This, I was thinking, was the life. I was two years into that contract and contemplating extending it. Italy, with its food and people, was all very much me. I was thirty-two years of age, an Edinburgh lad who'd been exported to England when I was just fifteen. A boy leaving his mum and dad and the rest of the family behind to set off on his football journey. Since then, I had served an apprenticeship at Spurs, there had been a transfer to Middlesbrough and then a move to Liverpool, where we were the dominant force in England and Europe. All of which led me to my time in Italy.

My early days in professional football seemed so long ago and so far away. The north London club of the late sixties and early seventies was a world away from what they are now. The first team was peppered with legends of the game like Jimmy Greaves, Martin Peters, Pat Jennings and the great Dave Mackay, who went to the same school as me. The side was so good they won the UEFA Cup. In those days – 1972 – it was over two legs, and Spurs defeated Wolverhampton in an all-English final.

Still, I was a kid in a hurry. I am not sure I could have spelled the word 'patience' back then. I was nineteen and, for me, life at Tottenham under Bill Nicholson was not moving quickly enough. Even at that age I was not shortchanged in the confidence department. I would approach the boss every Friday afternoon to ask why I was not in the first team. So, by January 1973, he had obviously had enough of my overly inflated ego and accepted an offer from Middlesbrough, a princely fee of £30,000.

Other clubs in London wanted to sign me but I reckon Bill Nicholson wanted me as far away from Tottenham as possible. So I was off to the northeast of England. The manager at Ayresome Park was Stan Anderson but I only played two games for him, an FA Cup tie against Plymouth that we lost and one against Fulham, which we also lost. He was sacked immediately afterwards.

Then, in May 1973, Jack Charlton took over. He made me grow up very quickly and realize what being a professional was all about. You listen to a guy with that kind of pedigree, who has won the World Cup and was so successful at Leeds United. He was ruthless and taught me so much about how to succeed at the highest level. My education in football was accelerating under Jack, and I was learning what kind of attitude you had to have to get to the very top of the game.

I had five happy years in the northeast before, in January 1978, Bob Paisley paid £352,000 – then a record fee between English clubs – for me to join Liverpool. Suddenly my life was on fire. Why such an odd number? Even in those days the rivalry between Liverpool and Manchester United was so big that the £2,000 was added to give Liverpool bragging rights over Manchester United, who had paid £350,000 for Joe Jordan!

I was now involved in one of the most ruthless professional environments in the UK and beyond. I was thrown into a different world. Ten minutes before my debut – West Brom at the Hawthorns – I foolishly asked the first-team coach, Joe Fagan, how he wanted me to play and I will never forget what he said.

'Fuck off. Listen, son. We have just paid all this money for you, and you are asking me how to play football?' said Joe, who despite that, I later realized, was a sympathetic ear and a kind of favourite uncle. He turned and walked away. And that was the first and last time I ever asked a question in my seven years at Anfield.

The mentality of the legendary boot room where coaches traditionally met at Liverpool was incredible. The team talks given by Bob Paisley, Ronnie Moran and Joe Fagan consisted of very few words – but every day at our training sessions they hammered home what was expected of us. They understood the game inside out, but they were also focused on its psychology and how to get the best out of each player. I look back at my education there and feel I attended the Oxbridge of football. It was not just that their football knowledge was second to none, their genius for keeping us on our toes every single day is something I tried to emulate right through my coaching career.

We won the English First Division title five times, but that was just the tip of the iceberg.

Three times we won Europe's premier competition. Liverpool almost had a monopoly on the European Cup at the time. And I became the club's proud captain. We were good. Really good. And with a Scottish core in me, Kenny Dalglish and Alan Hansen.

I didn't have a clue about it back then, but I would keep my Anfield education with me all my days.

Tales to be told there, right enough, but this is Italy in the spring of 1986. The phone call I am about to receive will change my life totally . . . the start of something that would forever alter not just Scottish football, but Scottish society too.

Scottish football was vastly different back then. It was a league filled with mostly domestic players, and, for the national team, World Cup qualification was almost guaranteed. Scotland was in the middle of a run which took them to every finals from 1974 to 1990 – five in a row. Furthermore, the Old Firm, Rangers and Celtic, were far from getting their own way. In fact, the headline writers had to give birth to the New Firm. Aberdeen and Dundee United from the east coast had a grip on most of the silverware and were making headlines in Europe. Glasgow Rangers in particular were struggling under the self-imposed burden of a shameful signing policy that was not only wrong but hampered their attempts to be successful.

Forty years on it seems inconceivable, but Glasgow Rangers, one of the most famous names in world football, would not sign Roman Catholics. So had Pelé, Diego Maradona and Lionel Messi knocked at the front door begging for a contract, they would have been told to sling their hook. I could never figure it out. Did they want a sectarian team or a successful one? From our vantage point in 2026, it seems nothing short of absolute madness.

I had left Liverpool after unprecedented success in English football. Not that I was finished yet. I had helped Sampdoria win the Italian Cup – the first trophy they had ever won – and now the owners fancied the Scudetto – the championship of Italy. I fancied a bit of that myself.

I had lived more than half my life outside the old country, although I was still a passionate Scot, with two World Cup campaigns in Argentina and Spain under my belt and a third in Mexico coming in a few months. Scots had played in Italy before – Denis Law for Torino in the sixties is the prime example. And Joe Jordan was at AC Milan and Verona just before I arrived at Sampdoria.

Nowadays, of course, Scottish international lads like Scott McTominay, Billy Gilmour and Lewis Ferguson – son of Derek, who played for me at Rangers – are out there playing in Serie A.

The globetrotting had brought me to the idyllic Italian seaside town of Nervi, along the coast from Genoa, the home of Sampdoria. I had a beautiful house and a garden that went all the way down to the Mediterranean. It had been a traditional fishing village but was now a chic small town with trendy boutiques and fabulous restaurants. Some claim that it was the birthplace of Christopher Columbus. I absolutely loved it. What a place to call home. It was a stunning setting. Lovely. *La dolce vita*. Nothing, I thought, can alter this course. Aye, very good, Graeme. I was to discover that life does not always work out the way you think it will.

Meanwhile, back in Scotland, there was a group of people planning a football revolution.

Edinburgh lad or not, my boyhood club had always

been Rangers, because that was who my brother Billy supported. And though I'd only represented clubs in England and Italy, I had always nurtured a deep affection for Glasgow's finest. I had played for Liverpool at Ibrox in a 2–0 victory – Kenny Dalglish and Ronnie Whelan scored – on 22 December 1981, in a game played to celebrate the completion of the redevelopment of the ground.

That was my first visit back there in a long time and I was extremely impressed with the shiny new stadium. It had exerted a hypnotic effect on me from the days when I was just a lad and Billy had taken me to European nights at Ibrox. Football under floodlights has always held a special magic for me. And back then Glasgow Rangers were the football kings of Scotland. Jimmy Millar and Ralph Brand, Jim Baxter, John Greig. A real football club. With a real working-class, dedicated and passionate support who inherited a love of the club that had run through generations of their families . . . and that still exists to this day.

Except, fast-forward into the early years of the eighties and it had become difficult to justify that claim of football superiority. Aberdeen and Dundee United – the by now well-branded New Firm – had nudged themselves alongside Celtic. Rangers had not won a title since 1978. It was a trophy desert. This had not been the Glasgow Rangers way. History dictated otherwise. And a massive club faced massive demands from a support who had known different and so much better times.

Jock Wallace had left in 1978 under mysterious circumstances – the truth of which he took to his grave, although there had been fallouts between him and his predecessor Willie Waddell – handing over to club legend John Greig as he headed for Leicester City.

It was an incredible summer of change for the Scottish game. Jock Stein finished his historic reign at Celtic and Alex Ferguson was sacked for the only time in his career – by St Mirren – before taking over at Aberdeen, the club Billy McNeill had left to inherit Jock's job at Parkhead. The domino effect rattled on as Ally MacLeod resigned as Scotland manager, to be replaced by Stein, whose spell succeeding Brian Clough at Leeds United had lasted just forty-four days. Keeping up?

Meanwhile Greigy, captain of the Rangers 1972 European Cup Winners' Cup-winning side, moved directly from the dressing room to the manager's office. Not easy. Trust me. Over the next five years, John, hampered by budget issues and a board who had lost their way, could not turn the club's fortunes around. One story that illustrates the darkness of this era for Rangers is that they tried to sign my Scotland teammate Willie Miller, then found that they could not match the wages he was earning at Aberdeen.

So it did not work for an absolute diamond of a man who would later, in 1986, resume a role as the beating heart of the club and the board, but who for now was flailing like a drowning man, reaching out for the lifeboat. In several directions.

They tried for Alex Ferguson, by this time conquering Europe with Aberdeen, but he rejected their advances because some weren't happy with the fact that his wife Cathy was a Roman Catholic. Rangers were steeped in Protestant culture. And people with Catholic connections just were not welcome at that time.

Ferguson said no and so did Jim McLean, then conjuring miracles with Dundee United, taking them to a league title and European Cup semi-final (a few years later, in 1987, they reached the UEFA Cup final). So they swallowed their humble pie and took back Big Jock, who had been coach to Willie Waddell when the club triumphed in Barcelona in 1972, winning what is still the only European trophy in the club's history. But this time it did not work. Rangers were struggling and the owner, Lawrence Marlborough, grandson of house-building tycoon John Lawrence, seemed like he was losing interest. Since 1963, John Lawrence (Glasgow) had been slowly increasing its shareholding in Rangers. Then, in November 1985, Marlborough, who had settled in Lake Tahoe in Nevada, took control of the club by purchasing the shares of the vice-chairman Jack Gillespie. This was the first time since the club had been incorporated as a company in 1899 that a single shareholder had obtained a majority of the shares and thus could be described as its owner.

Still, by 1985 then-chairman John Paton was describing Marlborough as a 'silent partner'. It was at this point that David Holmes – the new chairman and chief executive of the John Lawrence Group – entered the scene. By that time, he had helped turn John Lawrence into the largest independent house-builder in Scotland.

Holmes, who was rumoured to be a fan of his local team, Falkirk, did not lack self-confidence. But he had every right to have it. From humble beginnings he had worked hard to rise through the ranks of his trade. There were some in the press who did not fancy the cut of his jib. They were seriously misjudging the determination and single-mindedness of a man I would come to respect and admire. He believed that Rangers had – previously to the Lawrence Marlborough takeover – been run by a committee and were short on long-term planning. Now, having been given the power to redirect the route the club were going to take, he would go on to play an astonishing role in its rebirth. He overhauled the whole business of how Rangers were run, which meant that he would one day be able to unleash the funds that changed the marketplace for the club.

Rangers, finally, were on the move. They were to thrive by making their own income rather than being reliant on the largesse of the Lawrence empire. And one man understood that totally. Directors came and went but it was David Holmes who had the vision to see the way ahead.

By early April 1986 Holmes and the new Rangers administration had seen enough of Jock Wallace, and the trigger was pulled after only 12,000 fans turned up for a friendly against Spurs at Ibrox that the home team lost 2–0. It was a game that had only been arranged because Rangers were out of the Scottish Cup and the club had a free day.

This meant that Rangers had a vacancy for a manager, and David Holmes had decided to see if I'd be interested in becoming the first player-manager in Ibrox's history. At that precise moment, though, I was loving life in Italy. As I've already mentioned, I was a fan of the food, the people and the company I kept. And, of course, the football. Oh, and the wages were good and Sampdoria was run by brilliant guys. And the weather. In the north-west of England and in Scotland, sometimes you get lucky and the rain is warm. But the Italian Riviera. The very act of speaking it aloud inspires a smile.

In fact, I had just agreed with Paolo Mantovani – the president of Sampdoria and an absolute gentleman – to stay and complete the third year of my contract. Then the phone rang. No mobiles in those days and the internet was still the stuff of science fiction. This was a good old-fashioned landline. But, to be honest, the call was not totally unexpected.

The hint had come from the late football writer Ken Gallacher, who had phenomenal contacts in the game. I knew him well and trusted him. He tipped me off that Holmes was going to be making contact. And so the call was set up.

'My name is David Holmes. You don't know me, but I got your number from a mutual friend.' At that stage I had no ambitions or dreams about becoming a manager. Just never thought about it. But David Holmes's call intrigued me.

In fact, it mystifies me to this day. How, when, why and where my name was first mentioned is a mystery. I had no managerial experience, and I had not met anyone from the club. The Rangers board could have had no first-hand knowledge of my personality, although they must have asked several people about me. All they knew was that I had been captain of Liverpool and Scotland and was still playing at the highest level in Italy, with my third World Cup coming up.

Would one of these people who gave me a glowing reference have been Ken Gallacher? Ken has passed now, so we will never know. I was never even actually interviewed; I was simply offered the position with no reference to any other candidates, and can only assume that one morning Holmes woke up and said, 'What about Souness?'

It was, when I think back now, a real roll of the dice. It was David Holmes's light-bulb moment. Anyway, I was interested enough to agree to meet Holmes in a cloak-and-dagger operation.

The James Bond-style get-together happened at Milan Linate Airport, more than two hours' drive from Genoa and a long way from Glasgow. Holmes chatted to me for about two hours at Linate before reboarding the aircraft that had flown him in from Gatwick. The paparazzi did not get a sniff. Secrets seemed easier to keep back then in a pre-social-media world.

I liked what I'd heard from Holmes. There was already my childhood affection for the club, and my memories of those amazing European games at Ibrox. But more than that, it was a question of scale and intensity. The four clubs with the most passionate support in Britain are Liverpool, Manchester United, Rangers and Celtic. In London and elsewhere, football traditionally comes second. Fans of these four clubs live for Saturday. It is about tradition and the soul of the working man and woman. It is about history. It is about passion. That was true in 1986 and nothing I've seen since has changed my mind. So I knew Rangers were big. But the days still to come proved I had no idea how big. Or how global.

Out of nowhere, I was suddenly seduced into turning my life around. Sampdoria and the Mediterranean lifestyle were binned as I was wooed by the idea of managing and playing – for the first time – in Scottish football. It was as if I'd performed an emergency stop followed by a U-turn and had decided to take another route in my life without really analysing my decision.

And let me clear something up right now. Anyone who thinks that I moved to Rangers for the money is way off the mark. In fact, I took wages that were a third of what I was earning in Italy. It was a massive pay cut. Money was never the driver in all of this. It would have been more fruitful to stay at Sampdoria, where I could easily have extended my playing career. But then I do not have a good track record at choosing the easy options in life.

The truth is, I was bewitched. It was a remarkable turnaround. Four decades on, with the sanity of an older man, I wonder what was going through my 32-year-old mind. What I did know was that I was up for it. It was a risk, but one underpinned by the comfort of financial guarantees and a fund to build a team. These assurances came from David Holmes and I trusted this man would give me the keys to Ibrox. I hope history never underestimates what he achieved in the years after Lawrence Marlborough had the vision to see that this guy could do for a football club what he had done for a company that built houses.

My head was suddenly awash with enthusiasm and excitement, although on reflection I was naive in terms of what Rangers were all about. Scottish? Of course I was. In one sense I was like a foreigner, in that I had spent the last eighteen years out of the country, but my heart swelled with pride when I pulled on that dark blue jersey. Something lit a fire in my belly – I was captain of Scotland for heaven's sake. Maybe being picked to represent our country meant more to those of us who played down south. An English dressing room was a tricky place for Scots if you had just lost a game. But a grand place to strut your stuff if you had just recorded a win over them!

Anyway, I was still a Sampdoria player and was due to skipper my country at the forthcoming World Cup. My mind was whirling as I travelled back to the charming and lovely Nervi and my waiting family.

It was time for major decision-making. But deep in my heart I knew what I was going to do. I sensed something. If I did this, I was leaving behind wonderful Liguria for Scotland's industrial central belt and a daily hike between Edinburgh, where I intended to live, and Glasgow. I'd be walking out on a flourishing club that was on its way to being the best in Italy, and which soon would become champions, for a club that was wandering through some of its darkest days.

Glasgow Rangers needed some serious, challenging work. I was laying a lot on the line. But I decided to go for it. And I will never know how my life might have unfolded if I'd chosen otherwise. But deep inside, I knew from day one that I was never going to have a single regret. It was never in doubt that I would accept Rangers' offer.

From a fishing village to the Scottish goldfish bowl. You do not get to put an X in the 'no-publicity' box with Rangers. Glasgow is the biggest village in the world. Sometimes I think they invented the word 'gossip' there. The world wants to know and soon it did, with the tabloids and broadcast media in a feeding frenzy. In an ideal world, the announcement would have been kept past the end of the season in Scotland and Italy and until after the World Cup. Some chance . . . and when the dam leaks, the waters cascade.

I hoped we could keep the appointment under control, but by now the story was bursting at the seams. The stitching was about to surrender. And the rumour factory went into full production mode. So the club decided to announce it just twenty-four hours after the press conference announcing that Jock Wallace had left.

On Tuesday, 8 April 1986, the doors to the famous Blue Room at Ibrox Stadium were opened and I was ushered in as the club's first-ever player-manager, although I wouldn't start until the new season. Flashbulbs flared and I smiled at some of the faces of reporters I knew in the seated throng. I can tell you exactly what I said to them:

> It would sound corny if I said I supported Rangers as a boy, but I did. It is a fact. In football you can never rule anything out. I wanted to go into management, but I never expected such a big job, especially while I was still playing. Leaving a nice lifestyle does not come into it. I am a professional footballer and when I left Liverpool, I saw it as a step down, but this is a step up again.
>
> I am new to management and obviously there will be mistakes but I just hope they are not big ones. And I will not repeat them. The playing side of it is down to me. I knew after speaking with David Holmes I had to take the job. I would not have taken it if I did not feel it was right.

David then said that he was a fan of mine . . . and I replied saying that I hoped he still was in a year's time! What he did say to the media was this:

> I pencilled in where I wanted the club to go after being asked to come on to the board and the only name I could get into my mind was Graeme Souness. I felt if this club was ambitious then this club had to go for the very best and Graeme *is* the very best. I am absolutely delighted. I have a lemon here in my pocket and I suck it every now and then to help wipe the smile off my face!

Excuse me while I blush. And we were off and running. It was the greatest show in town.

Earlier this year it was the fortieth anniversary of that day and – not that I am big on following it – I was astonished by how many people on social media acknowledged the occasion. It is more than half my lifetime ago, but supporters who were around to witness it all, and the subsequent generations who have been told the tale, still recall it.

I sat in the dugout for the last game of the season – a 2–0 win over Motherwell that was to secure us a European place. There were just 21,500 fans at Ibrox that day. By the next week – a Friday night because the Scottish Cup final between Aberdeen and Hearts was the following day – I had won my first trophy. In front of 40,000 at Ibrox, Ally McCoist scored a hat-trick to help us win a 3–2 extra-time victory over Celtic in the Glasgow Cup final. In truth, I had not started the job, because it was still the old season, but who doesn't love a glory hunter? And my appointment had been announced!

So rose the dawn on the most astonishing five years of my life, in which the culture of Scotland changed course, we flushed down the toilet a signing policy that had shamed the club's history for a century and more, and we breathed new life into a football institution. It was five years in which newspapermen rubbed their hands with joy and the Rangers support faced up to head-spinning levels of change and success. Maybe I should have called this book *Never a Dull Moment*. Because in the years ahead there was not a single one. The adventure was off and running.

Now, if I can just say something here.

2

Let's Talk About Walter

It was a one-horse race. Not another runner and rider in sight.

In truth, I had not even considered that I might need an assistant manager. It was David Holmes who suggested the concept when he asked, 'What's your relationship like with Walter Smith?' The name of the only candidate that there ever was. And it was David who made it happen. After Jock Wallace left, his assistant, Alex Totten, briefly took the reins, and later I would hear it whispered that big Jock was interested in staying on with me in some kind of advisory role, but that suggestion never got as far as me at the time and I never got to meet the man. Instead, well before I arrived at the club to take up my position, we agreed that we wanted Walter Smith to join us from Dundee United, where he was assistant manager to Jim McLean.

But there was a snag. Jim McLean did not want him to

leave Tannadice. More than that, the club were demanding a fee of £50,000 for their assistant manager who – as Walter himself pointed out – as a player had once been sold by McLean to Dumbarton for £7,000 and then bought back for £3,000 less! That was some increase in valuation for someone who was not even a player any more.

Walter suggested to David Holmes that he did not think United had any right to ask for compensation . . . but this was the new Rangers, and everything was handled with style. Our man – according to Walter – picked up the phone, called the Dundee United chairman George Fox, and simply asked where the cheque for fifty grand should be sent. He then had it couriered to Fox's house in Carnoustie that evening so that Walter could start immediately.

Walter was irked at the way his old club had treated him after twenty years of service, but he realized at once how much Rangers valued him. On reflection, United rated him highly too, and maybe they knew what they were losing. David spoke with him, then I did, and I could hear the enthusiasm in his voice. He was gloriously excited. Here was a man about to be delivered his dream. In fact, this was maybe something that, as a young player and a manager, he had never even dared to dream. And so one of the finest human beings I have ever known came into my world.

I did not know much about Walter Smith, beyond his role with McLean at Dundee United, where he had once played, and who were now, alongside Aberdeen, ruling the roost in Scotland. And, of course, I knew him from getting together on Scotland duty, where Alex Ferguson trusted him completely. But we instantly clicked, and then our relationship as pals, and as people who understood and loved the game, deepened. Till the day he died, he insisted the five years we had together were the best of his professional life. I was to learn that he was an incredibly special man.

Dear, wonderful Walter Smith. He was fabulous for me. I was a hothead. And I was completely raw as a manager. Walter was a diamond of a human being. He was grounded, and as someone who was Rangers to the core, and understood exactly what the club was all about, he taught me so much. I had left Scotland at the age of fifteen but he, who knew the Scottish game inside out, had never worked south of the border, and would not until decades later, when he left for Everton. He ticked all the boxes as the number two I never knew I needed. Although I was still a Sampdoria player until the current season ended, and there was a spaghetti of relationships all over the place, as the first campaign at Ibrox beckoned, Walter and I were already side by side. We were a perfect fit for one another.

I thought I knew what to expect at the club, but the truth is I had no idea. Walter taught me the magnitude of Rangers. The passion he warned me about was way beyond anything I had ever experienced. When he arrived, David Holmes had sacked the entire backroom staff and so the Ibrox dressing room we came to know was a vastly different place. Walter found that even the training kit was a shambles, with the players picking their gear from a pile in the centre of the floor, putting it on, and going to work. Sometimes, after a morning in the pouring rain at the Albion training ground on Broomloan Road across from the stadium, the players would walk back to the changing room and dump their kit on the floor again. The balls were old and scuffed and left with the kit in the changing room, and the ground-staff boys – there were only two of them apparently – were nowhere to be seen.

The following day, we'd arrive to find that first thing in the morning the gear had been put away on hangers in the old-fashioned drying rooms, having spent the night on the dressing room floor. But it had not been washed first! The kit was rigid with dried-out dirt.

It was ridiculous. Rangers were trailing what was happening at other clubs. The standards at Ibrox were way behind what I had been used to at Liverpool and in Italy. It was an absolute joke. Where we trained had to be seen to be believed. Every morning when we turned up at the single pitch, it was clear that kids had been playing on it at night. There were supermarket trolleys, rubbish and dog mess lying about. This was Glasgow Rangers and yet the facilities would have embarrassed an amateur club. Everything had been ignored for years. Laundry facilities, equipment, basics. Our training kit, balls, in fact all the stuff we needed, were a disgrace. I wanted my players to feel special and these facilities sure were not doing the job.

Many years later, the club built the state-of-the-art centre in Milngavie on the other side of the river, but, at the time, I tried and failed to get them to buy Moore Park, which was the home of Scottish Junior Football Association club St Anthony's and lay a few hundred yards from Ibrox on Edmiston Drive. I did not want reserve games played on the Ibrox surface because the football I was asking the players to play required the ball to be on the grass more than they were used to. The revolution had to start with the basics. It was breathtaking how bad it was.

Never underestimate the magnitude and the passion of the Rangers family and what the club means to people throughout the world. Walter never did. He was a Rangers man through and through, and he helped me understand the importance of the small and big decisions at Ibrox. He had grown up in Carmyle, in the East End of Glasgow, and from day one he was steeped with the Rangers way.

In truth, he did not set the world on fire as a player, but he was highly rated as a coach, first by Jim McLean at Tannadice, but also by Andy Roxburgh, who appointed him as his assistant with the youth team. In fact, together they won the 1982 European Under-18 Championship in Finland, still the only professional tournament Scotland has ever captured. It was clear that he was officer material.

A curious twist of fate threw us together as part of the Scotland squad for the 1986 World Cup finals in Mexico and the pre-tournament altitude training in Santa Fe, New Mexico. I got to know him there, me as the team's captain and him as assistant to Alex Ferguson, who had stepped in after the tragic passing of Jock Stein, who had died leading his nation as far as a play-off tie against Australia.

I have heard cynics whisper otherwise, but on that trip we always put Scotland first. Yes, there was a lot of down time in which we discussed the upcoming job at Rangers, but the Mexico campaign was always head of the queue.

It was love at first sight. He watched and listened and always showed me respect, and I instantly liked him. From day one there was a real fondness. With Walter, what you saw was what you got, and he was a genuinely good man. You just knew he spoke the truth at every turn. He had a particular way about him. And when he accepted the job, he knew – we all did – that he had come home. His blood ran blue. His heroes were the team of the sixties, and he had a particular affection for Jimmy Millar, centre forward for that side and one half of a legendary partnership with Ralph Brand. He even got to play with Millar when the old Rangers warhorse wound down his career at Dundee United.

Walter and I were vastly different characters and personalities in one sense, but the relationship worked immediately. I could be like a bull in a china shop, while he found it hard to upset people. He would handle things in different ways to me. But, despite the differences, we had business to do. A squad to assemble. It was time to go shopping.

The day I arrived at Ibrox for my unveiling was the first time I'd been back since that Liverpool friendly in 1981. But I quickly got Walter to arrange a game with the squad on the pitch so we could assess what we had. I remember thinking that some were good and some were not, which was no real surprise for me because the previous manager had lost his job with the players he had. I had already realized it was going to be a big challenge.

Walter knew the players at Rangers and in Scotland generally and I did not. In particular, he was of course *au fait* with the staff at Dundee United and we knew we had to get Richard Gough, a magnificent athlete with a 100 per cent committed approach to his career. From the first time I came across him in the Scotland squad I'd known he was the real deal. We tried a bid of £650,000 – a massive sum back then – but we failed. What we learned, quickly, was that clubs in Scotland were not keen on selling to Rangers, and wee Jim McLean – who, remember, had years earlier declined the manager's role at Ibrox – was particularly stubborn in that department. So, there is a curious thing: Walter Smith could have been Rangers' assistant manager with Jim, not me!

We also wanted Maurice Malpas, an exceptionally talented utility player, but again Jim McLean would not let the chain tying him to break, no matter the pressure we applied. He did not let him go . . . ever. Mo stayed with Dundee United his entire career and ended up chalking up an unbelievable 830 appearances for his club. We would get Gough eventually, the best signing I ever made, though it had to come via the scenic route.

Just as the likes of Liverpool and Manchester United and Chelsea and Manchester City now have to pay a premium when they sign players from other English clubs, Rangers had to pay a premium when we signed from our Scottish rivals. The price would always go up for us. What had happened in the past was this: an inflated fee would be paid over three or four years, and if the player wasn't cutting it, the last two payments were binned and the player could return to his club. This happened because no one in Scotland liked us and there was a threat that if Rangers got it right then we would steamroll everyone in the country bar Celtic.

Walter knew every player in Scotland, but we eventually agreed that most of our shopping would be south of the border. The vast majority of my knowledge was about the English leagues, where I had played for sixteen years. I knew the players down south and I knew we could get at them, because of our war chest and because English clubs were being denied access to European football after the five-year ban that had been imposed in the wake of the Heysel Stadium disaster, which had led to the deaths of thirty-nine and hundreds of injuries. It allowed us to reverse the tide that had always swept Scotland's top players south. English players in their pomp faced a career devoid of appearing in Europe, so suddenly we could make the river flow north. And we sure did.

But that is how partnerships work. Immediately, I understood that Walter and I had the same mentality but had separate ways of showing it. Not that I always got it right. An agent friend of mine, Pini Zahavi, recommended Ronny Rosenthal, an Israeli striker who was playing in Belgium. We had him in Glasgow for a week and we had a right good look at him: he was lightning quick and could score goals. But I thought the Scottish game would be too aggressive for him, that he was not strong enough, so we did not pursue him. As it happens, he went on to build a reputation at Liverpool, so I must admit with hindsight that I got that one horribly wrong.

There was another player who had recently left Scotland to play in England, someone who would eventually become assistant manager at Ibrox: Gary McAllister. He had moved to Leicester City from Motherwell, and I went to see him at Swindon one sunny afternoon. That day he was head and shoulders above everyone else on a very bobbly pitch. Walter was familiar with him from his days in Scotland and knew that he was a Rangers fan. We did not pursue him for the same reasons as Rosenthal. I believed that the aggression faced by Rangers players would be too much for him. Looking back, he was another one who slipped through the net. He would have been fabulous for us because he got better as he got older, to such an extent that he became captain of Scotland, won fifty-seven caps, and ended his career at Liverpool. And of course, when Steven Gerrard became boss at Ibrox, Gary was his number two. We took our eyes off the ball with that one.

I arrived at Rangers with a massive profile, but Walter going into his boyhood club did not change him or his approach to the game one iota. He was engaging and funny, with a dry sense of humour. He had a wonderful way of disagreeing and I was never aware of us falling out, even when we made decisions that were not popular with some of the supporters, the players, the media or the Scottish Football Association. Or any other club.

Walter and I were vastly different characters, but we were always in agreement. Eventually!

I would walk away from discussions thinking I had won until I reflected about it and thought to myself, 'Hang on a minute!' Oh, he was good, all right. Whatever we did was aimed at making Glasgow Rangers better. Our target was to win trophies not popularity competitions.

Walter did not have an illustrious career as a player, but he could hold his own in our six- or eight-a-side games in training and used to whip me in penalty competitions. He was good at that too. Although I have a sneaking feeling that Chris Woods tried harder with my efforts.

Our first signing was striker Colin West from Watford for £200,000, but Woods, then the England number two to Peter Shilton, was the first high-profile one. He first came into my orbit soon after I arrived at Liverpool, when I was cup-tied for the 1978 League Cup final at Wembley against Nottingham Forest, in which he was outstanding. It was a draw, and in the replay at Old Trafford he was again brilliant. Forest won it with a penalty from my late, great and dear friend John Robertson, who I had known since the late sixties and the Scotland schools' team. On the night the story broke about Woods joining us, he was on the bench for England in a World Cup tie against Morocco in Monterrey in Mexico, although he would go on to become his nation's first choice.

With our first signings, we had made it clear that anyone was now fair game for the Rangers cheque book. Meanwhile, as my managerial career was taking off, I was also playing my last games for Scotland, with Walter looking on as part of the coaching team. I hated how it all ended. Scotland lost to Denmark and West Germany, and I played in both games, but I let myself down in these matches and I know why. I had food poisoning and ended up a stone – six and a half kilos or so – under my playing weight by the end of the second game. I was weak as a kitten.

Alex Ferguson dropped me for the remaining game – versus Uruguay – and even though I had never been left out of a team in my life, I accepted that I had been nowhere near good enough to play in the final group fixture. There were legitimate reasons for my staying out of the game. Ferguson eventually confessed he was wrong to leave me out of a match we had to win. He had wanted to use me as a substitute, but I refused to even be on the bench.

The game was a physical battle, and the South Americans were an extremely aggressive team. When José Batista was sent off in the first minute, it was clear how Uruguay were going to go about this. The thing is, I was an experienced player and well trained in the dark arts of the game. Normally in a fixture of such physicality and aggression I would have been perfect, but I knew I was not up to it. In any case, with me looking on, Uruguay hung on for the 0–0, which put us out of the tournament.

In retrospect, Scotland also got the timing of their altitude training all wrong. Sports science has proven that to be the case, and curiously it was my club who benefitted. The advantages of coming back to sea level post-Mexico were triggered in the hard yards of preseason. I was by far the fittest in our squad at Rangers, and that was largely due to the altitude work on the other side of the Atlantic.

In any case, I had made up my mind – after three World Cup finals and fifty-four caps – not to play for my country again. I strived to make it clear it was nothing to do with any huff about being dropped for the last game. It was all to do with the enormity of the challenge ahead. I had made the decision that this would be my last tour on national duty before flying to the tournament. The demands of the new job and the fact that I had a young family to attend to meant that my days of finishing work at lunchtime were over.

After we were eliminated in Mexico, we flew to Gatwick and I continued to Majorca, where my family were based, so I could see the kids: Chantelle, Fraser and Jordan, who was born in Genoa. They would continue to live there when I moved to Scotland to start at Ibrox. But even in Spain I was on the phone to Walter at least twice a day as we laid out our plans. There was much work to be done, and we were going to do it together.

Meanwhile, I chose not to move to Glasgow. Instead, I moved in with my dad James – my mum Elizabeth had died two years earlier – in his council house in Saughton Mains in Edinburgh.

I ended up being there for more than a year while I had a house built in Colinton, a genuinely nice area in the capital. My company car was a brand-new plush and shiny Jaguar, and I recall it sat happily outside that council house without a single issue.

Mind you, while I was staying at my dad's I nearly lost more than my car. My life. One weekend, Andy Roxburgh – by then the Scotland manager – invited me, as the former captain of the national team, to Gleneagles to spend some time with the squad, who had gathered there. While I was there, I got a phone call at 2 a.m. from my brother saying: 'Don't panic, but there has been a fire at Dad's house.' Tragically, an old lady downstairs had died in her flat, and my old man would have been a victim had a man, who curiously enough was out walking a cat on a lead, not noticed the smoke and raised the alarm. While I did not lose my life, what I did lose was my wardrobe of very exclusive and expensive Versace gear, which all went up in smoke.

Meanwhile, being with Walter every day was a joy. We were desperate to get to work, and as I was speeding along the M8 each morning, all the focus was on the job at hand. When we were together, he was just brilliant. My tastes in terms of food, fashion and drinking had been honed in Italy, so I made Walter learn! I was into pasta and fine wine. Wattie did admit at the time: 'I was a mince and tatties man until I met Graeme!' He also had a desperate fashion sense. He wore old man gear, and I used to rib him about it, saying: 'You're not coming out with me dressed like that.' But he took it well and upped his game.

Based on my time in Italy, I also made slight changes to the playing squad's routines. I told Walter one day that I wasn't stupid, that I knew we couldn't stop the players from going out on a Saturday night, and that when they inevitably did they were not going to be drinking soft drinks. But I asked: 'Walter, is this daft? Tell them to sit down when they are having a drink. It is a better look for a professional footballer than standing at the bar sinking pints.' He agreed, so he mentioned it to the players. We bounced off one another. We were a good team.

I also made them wear flip-flops as they came out the showers, because doing so lowers the risk of picking up an infection and protects a footballer's feet against anything that might be lying on the floor. Common sense. Plus I insisted to David Holmes that we needed new pressurized showers in the changing rooms that gave more hot water. I remember the cost . . . £18,000, a fair sum back then. But, as always, he left no stone unturned. He was supportive to the hilt and he got it done.

The other thing is that we banned them from playing golf. I play a lot now, which has confirmed to me that I was 100 per cent correct. If you play too near a match day you are taking something out of your legs. You lose a bit of your edge. It is about small margins in football, and you need all the strength you have for matches. You are a professional, and football – your job – should be your priority.

I benefitted so much from those five years with Walter at the club, and also beyond Rangers. We were a formidable partnership, but he was such a nice man. A wonderful human being. He had a separate way from me. I was too tough with people, but that was down to how I had been educated in the Liverpool dressing room. He got his message across in a gentler way. No one had a bad word to say about him. No one. And that proves the effectiveness of his way.

He even got respect from the East End of Glasgow, and it was not just to do with carrying Tommy Burns's coffin after the former Celtic manager, who was also Walter's assistant when he was Scotland manager, passed away. Walter crossed the divide.

And he was fun. Walter loved the camaraderie of the dressing room, the wind-ups and the jokes. We used to play six- or eight-a-side on a Friday morning and if it was Scotland versus England, I played for the other mob . . . for no other reason than that 'the Jocks', as the English players called them, refused to pick me. The games could get tasty. Walter was the referee. Usually it was Ally McCoist or Ray Wilkins who would cause the problem with their verbals, but one day, with me not being quite as fast as I once was, Ian Durrant nutmegged me and I took a lunge at him. 'Is that the best you've got?' he said, as he bounced back to his feet.

'No,' I said, and took a jab at him. Players from each side were now exchanging blows and Wattie abandoned the game while trying to separate battling teammates. The players thought all hell would break loose when I got back to the dressing room. It was, after all, Friday, the day before a match. But later, as they sat quietly in the dressing room, I opened the door and said: 'Brilliant. That's the attitude I'm looking for. Battling for your teammates. Well done. Let us see it tomorrow.' They were stunned. The next day? Eh, if my memory serves me right, we lost 2–0.

That was not Walter's only time as peacemaker, though. I remember we were on a flight, and I had this lovely three-quarter-length cream-coloured raincoat that I had just bought. I folded it carefully and put it in the overhead locker before sitting down in my window seat. Then this clown comes up and throws his manky old briefcase on my coat and I am trying to get at him as my assistant is holding me back! I could be a bit excitable back then.

Although there was a bit of role reversal in our Italian preseason camp at Il Ciocco years later, when a recently appointed official at the club tried to take pictures of chairman David Murray's son, who was slightly inebriated at the time. This time I was the restrainer and Walter the restrained as the red mist came down.

Those early days were exciting. Walter and I consulted on everything, and I still felt I had something to offer as a player, which meant that if I was on the pitch for a game he was the manager. It was his call who to substitute . . . as long as it was not me, of course. I trained hard and played hard but also made sure I headed back to Majorca every second weekend to see the family, leaving Ibrox as fast as I could after a game. After the quickest shower and an even quicker few words with the press, it was a race down the M8 to the airport and the Palma-bound flight. All that for not much more than a day with my kids.

I had to adapt to life back in Scotland and I had to be educated about the domestic game. I used to be impressed with some of the players who came up against us, and we would then go and watch them in matches against other teams to see if that was their normal level. But then I realized that they had raised their game because they were Rangers or Celtic fans and wanted to impress for differing reasons. In other games we watched, they were far inferior players to the personalities they had shown playing against us.

That was the difference. If you play for Rangers there are no easy games. Or at least you can make them into easy games, but only after the shift is done and you have shown why you are at the club. Players at other clubs, when they get the fixtures, mark down the games against Rangers and Celtic as special days. Which means that at Ibrox every game needs to be played at peak level. Every game either Rangers or Celtic are involved in is a cup final for the clubs they face, so mentally you must be ready for that every time you cross the white line. If the players could not handle that pressure, then I would show them the door. I needed winners and competitors like Terry Butcher, Mark Hateley, Richard Gough and Terry Hurlock, who all eventually ended up at Rangers.

I did not mess about in the middle of the park either, but sometimes I felt I was treated unfairly, and Walter would give me a heads-up about who would be having a look at me. Usually he got it right. But there was once a wee mix-up on the information highway on, of all games, my debut. It was a hot Saturday afternoon at Easter Road on 9 August 1986, with 24,576 packed into the ground for a game against Hibs. It seemed as if the eyes of the world were on us. And this was my hometown. The media attendance was huge, with their big guns coming up from England. We were massive news: new manager, new players, new season to prove ourselves the champions we could be.

What happened next was your perfect example of an inglorious beginning. Referee Mike Delaney produced a deserved straight red card after just thirty-six minutes for an assault by me on a Hibs player. It was a case of mistaken identity. And it was all Walter's fault. Believe me, 100 per cent. And here is the evidence for the prosecution. We had, of course, prepared thoroughly for my debut. But this was in the days before names on jerseys, and at the last minute – as the buzzer from the referee went in the dressing room and we were about to leave – Walter suddenly shouted across the room that he knew a player from his Dundee United days who, he said, 'was likely to leave one on you'. 'It's Kirkie,' he said. The player in question was Billy Kirkwood.

'Who's Kirkie?' I asked, and what was his number? Wattie couldn't tell me. I knew who it was *not* because my old mate Alan Rough was in goal for them. But it could have been any of the other ten. Essentially I was thinking:

I'm playing ten Billy Kirkwoods. Which is why I ended up assaulting George McCluskey.

The retaliate-first plan had gone horribly wrong and every player on the park, bar Scotland teammate Alan Rough, gathered in a centre-circle rammy. A 'stramash' may be the term. Roughie never fancied that kind of nonsense. And actually he was already on a booking after protesting about the penalty we had been awarded earlier in the match. He preferred watching while leaning on his post. Anyway, I got my marching orders, and probably because of that we lost my debut match.

I believe every single player, bar Rough, was retrospectively booked for the battle in the middle of the pitch. Even our goalkeeper, Chris Woods, sprinted half the length of the pitch to get involved in the fracas. McCluskey later successfully appealed against his caution given that he was lying prostrate at the time. Fair enough.

My red card was the beginning of an interesting and expensive relationship with the SFA, which lasted the next five years. The thing that I will never forget is the sight of my father sitting in the front row of the directors' box, in the stadium where he used to sneak in as a kid, looking on. It was one of the lowest moments of my career. My dear, wonderful dad, who never laid a finger on me and was the nicest, most relaxed man on the planet. My mum had a similar nature and never hit me . . . although she might have thrown a few things at me. I think she was also disappointed, given I was the third boy, that I was not a girl! But my point is this. How on earth did I get my temperament?

Hibs won the game 2–1 with goals from Steve Cowan and Stuart Beedie, although it had been 1–1 when I got my marching orders (we had scored via the Ally McCoist penalty that Roughie had argued about). But out of the darkness I took strength from the unity and spirit of our team – the fact that all the players rushed to show how united we were. Not great optics for the purists, but it did really produce a sign of better days to come. The best of it was that, as I marched up the tunnel, the man in the dugout who had triggered the mayhem and was 100 per cent guilty was tut-tutting and shaking his head . . . Walter!

But on reflection it was an early lesson for me in terms of teams raising their game for matches against the Old Firm. Hibernian won that day, but we went on to win the league. The Easter Road club finished ninth in a twelve-club division and won only nine more games in their season's forty-four fixtures. To win championships you must churn it out every single week and other clubs were not capable of doing that.

How I miss Walter. To this day. We had a fabulous working relationship and man-on-man friendship, and the illness that killed him was an evil thing. Just dreadful. Walter was wonderful company and he loved wonderful company. At times he could be like a schoolboy having fun. That house in Helensburgh and his love for and from his wife Ethel and his two lads made him one of the most grounded human beings I have ever met in the mad world of football. I never saw him down, but if he ever was, Ethel – his childhood sweetheart – would have had him bouncing back. I still think about him a lot.

The last time I saw him was in his house. He was in bed, attached to an oxygen tube and, I think, a saline drip. I sat on a two-seater couch in the room, but he insisted that he got out of bed and came – despite his weakness – to sit as close to me as he could, so that we were touching each other. Looking back, it was his way of saying goodbye. It broke my heart. He passed away just a few days later, in October 2021.

Walter Smith was fearless, and despite his ferocious love of his club he knew things had to change. I made it clear before the 1986 World Cup that I was prepared – no, insisted on – signing a high-profile Roman Catholic, thus blowing to smithereens a signing policy that was hampering the club's progress. He backed me all the way, as he always did, and when the great moment came and I revealed to him who we were going to sign his reaction was classic Walter. There were twenty seconds of silence, and he puffed out his cheeks. And then he said, 'Fuckin' hell, let's do this.'

So I said: 'OK, let's go to Edinburgh and you can tell the chairman about your idea!' I can even now see the expression on his face!

Oh, Walter. It was a partnership carved in heaven, and I will never forget those days of the mid- to late eighties and very early nineties. I was proud to call you my friend, proud of what we achieved for Glasgow Rangers. I think I was good for you . . . but that sure worked the other way too. We diverted history together; gave a rebirth to the football club you adored all your life. And you went on to manage it twice. As well as your country. That stands for a life well lived and fulfilled. Together we won four championships and four League Cups and took Rangers back where they belonged. Walter Ferguson Smith OBE was the most special of men. It was the most special of times.

3

Get the Motor Running

It was spooky but totally innocent.

In a television interview in September 1985, I had made the throw-away remark that I would not mind being manager of Rangers one day, adding that the man who turned around Glasgow Rangers would be forever remembered. I had been at a Scotland gathering where I was interviewed for the BBC Scotland documentary *Only a Game?* There was no grand thinking or scheming behind it. I don't even remember why I uttered the line – maybe it was because the club's form had been the subject of pre-interview chat. But who knows, maybe David Holmes heard it, and it affected his thinking? Maybe the seed was planted, but a cunning plan it was not. It sure was not a 'come and get me, Rangers'.

Fate has always seemed to intervene with me. As I look back, I do acknowledge that it has been no ordinary existence. My first brush with fame was when I broke through at Middlesbrough and I cannot honestly say I disliked it. Of course, it opened doors for a young man.

I have lived in the public eye for a long time and travelled the football world. But Rangers and Glasgow were something else. Not in Liverpool, nor even in Istanbul where I later managed Galatasaray, nor in Lisbon when I managed Benfica, did I get stuck in traffic jams and have people gesturing to me from the car in the next lane. But I sure did as I hit the gridlock on the M8 coming into Glasgow. The city's passion for football is unmatched. Perhaps even a wee bit unhinged at times.

In any case, fate had played its hand and here I was, in charge of the club I supported as a kid, although I never went to Saturday games then. I was too busy playing for my the school in the morning and Tynecastle Boys Club in the afternoon.

Like my two older brothers before me, every night after my tea I would catch the bus and go to stay with my grandmother in a tenement flat in Gorgie near Hearts' ground – though I was never a fan. She had felt lonely since my grandad died and hated being on her own, so I would catch the bus back home in the morning to pick up my bag before heading to school.

My dad was a Hibs man and he told me tales of how he used to sneak into Easter Road with his pals at night and play on the pitch. Can you imagine that now? But my brother Billy was a big Rangers fan and went to European midweek games at Ibrox, taking me with him, and obviously that did affect my thinking. It was there I fell in love with the enormity and the passion of the club. I sensed something about the place even then. Football hooked me incredibly early in life.

Anyway, there was work to be done. Players to be signed and statements of intent to be made. Rangers had invested heavily in the previous years in upgrading the stadium, which had had to be ripped apart after the Ibrox disaster of 1971, when sixty-six fans lost their lives at the end of an Old Firm game. The infamous hell of Stairway 13. Those poor souls.

The tragedy made the government investigate the safety of sports grounds in an inquiry that was led by Lord Wheatley – a judge at the time. Rangers started three years of reconstruction work and by its completion there were three new all-seated stands with – by 1981 – a capacity of 44,000. The stadium was magnificent and we were a decade ahead of what was happening down south, where the demand for all-seater stadiums was just catching up. This much-needed investment nevertheless impacted the club's activity in the transfer market, so they did not spend a lot of money. By the time I joined, they had been in the wilderness way too long. But now we needed to get this show on the road.

I needed big players who understood the mission. I needed guys who could still play their best football when all the pressure was being heaped upon them. Ordinary Joes did not cut it at this club. Only real men would do. You need to rise above the anxiety and the fear factor when you play for Rangers, more than anywhere else. Being second in the league – even playing the best football – is failure in Scotland. This brings incredible pressure. One bad result can cause you to lose the top spot, and that brings all the criticism and negative pressure to bear. You need to be mentally tough to play for RFC.

That first summer, I was constantly reminded about the size of the club and its support. We went to London to play a preseason friendly against Spurs at White Hart Lane in a testimonial for Paul Miller. Around 10,000 of our supporters turned up for a friendly 400 miles away – a fact that my pal Paul remains incredibly grateful for. It was astonishing.

That the momentum was building was underlined by the fact that the club's annual general meeting, which normally was held in the members' suite at the stadium, had to be postponed and rehoused in the Scottish Exhibition and Conference Centre. When they had tried it on the original date, shareholders had been because of the volume of attendance. We were attracting more people to meetings than some clubs were to games. We had certainly stirred something.

I wanted players who understood that it was no good winning the championship and then handing it back to Celtic the following year, the two of us alternating as title winners. I wanted a period of dominance. The most abused word in football these days is 'legend', tagged to players who maybe scored twenty goals in a one-off season. Good, but legend? And put on that pedestal? Give me a break. Where does that leave players like Phil Neal, my old Liverpool teammate, who won four European Cups, eight league titles, four League Cups and one Super Cup? There is a man worthy of the noun. In the game right now, there are nobodies earning wages that will have a generational effect. What they are putting in their pockets will secure the lifestyles of their grandchildren.

It was so different back then. We had truly great players. We had bought ourselves Chris Woods . . . although the historians will want to point out that the first name in was Colin West from Watford for £200,000. Mind you, if you are being really pernickety, in a sense my first real signing was Ally McCoist on a four-year contract extension. I made sure all the players who I was retaining were taken care of. Now we had West and Woods, it was time to go for even bigger fish.

Terry Butcher was captain of Ipswich Town and England. We took the spine of their national team and put it in our club. Their goalkeeper and centre half. I had played against Terry Butcher many times. He was brave, knowledgeable and maybe the best central defender on the planet. I knew if we could get him, he would be *the* statement. So, I set out on the mission. First of all, we agreed a fee of £750,000 with Ipswich Town, and they gave us permission to speak to him.

I phoned him. Nowadays, directors of football contact the player's agent and go from there, but because of the asset value, players hold all the aces. The Alexander Isak situation was a case in point. He successfully held Newcastle to ransom. I don't criticize him because I did it with Middlesbrough when I knew Liverpool wanted me. To be fair, it never happened to us at Ibrox because we created a monster and we became an extremely attractive proposition for the big players in the UK. Spurs and Manchester United wanted Terry, but I knew he was the key to my plans.

I spoke to him in the UK on the phone and again afterwards in Los Angeles, where he was captaining a Rest of the World Select XI. The match was for UNICEF and was being played in the Rose Bowl in Pasadena, and Big Tel scored. He was in a merry mood after the game and, given the chat, I think he had had a couple of sherbets.

He agreed to meet me at the Marriott Hotel at Heathrow after he touched down, so I headed for London. I waited for an hour or so in the hotel, but there was no sign of him, then suddenly it dawned on me that there were two Marriotts at the airport. I quickly phoned the other one and asked the concierge if Terry Butcher was there; he confirmed that he was. 'Put him on,' I said. I told Tel not to move and headed there.

The next thing was to get him to Glasgow, where he could see the stadium and the passion of the fans. He was a bit reluctant and disbelieving because, as captain of England, the city had not always opened its arms to him. However, I persuaded him to take the next flight north before he went home after his lengthy transatlantic journey. Once Terry was in Scotland I whisked him to the stadium. This is what I would almost always end up doing with players I wanted to sign, because the sight of Ibrox was a persuasive factor.

I also leaked the story that Terry was on his way to Ibrox to a journalist, and hundreds of fans turned up to welcome him. That changed everything, as he had a warm reception from some of our fans, on top of him seeing the ground that – as I said – was state of the art at the time. I did not fail to sign a single player who came to see the ground. I always made certain there was a welcome committee of fans, just to make sure. But the ground was fabulous. And Terry realized that.

His wife Rita flew north the next day and then the great man signed. Terry grew to love his life in Scotland, settling in the picturesque little town of Bridge of Allan and driving the miles to the city every day. Over the years, a lot of the English players we brought north also grew to love the country and stayed on.

I cannot underestimate the effect he had. Terry was the catalyst for everything we achieved at Rangers. He was a talented player and a wonderful character and a leader of men. He did my job on the park for me. Few players for me were better, on or off the pitch. It was £750,000 of fabulous bargain. Players like him have confidence in their own ability and do not shirk responsibility when the going gets tough. They are not all like that.

And yet . . . in all the time Chris Woods spent at Rangers – and that was from 1986 all the way through to 1991 – no player put more goals past him than . . . Terry Butcher. The big man was king of the own goals! But that was maybe because he put himself in where it hurt. Some players will hide and keep themselves out of harm's way, which makes them more cautious and less prone to mistakes, but you could not be like that at RFC. My team did not do that. I was proud of the squad we were building. We searched everywhere for talent, and the club was a force to be reckoned with in the transfer marketplace.

Butcher was extraordinary for Rangers, and I always regret the circumstances under which he eventually left the club in 1990, after 127 appearances. He was carrying an injury, and I told him not to talk about it, particularly to STV, whom I had banned because of their treatment of me and the football club. But after I told Terry my feelings about our fallout with them, I saw him from the manager's office doing a television interview with one of their reporters on the central reservation outside the stadium. We fell out over that and he moved to Coventry – yes, we fell out and I sent him there – where he played just a handful of games. But that hatchet was well and truly buried years back.

I was learning quickly as I went about the work of building the club. After I joined Rangers, and on just the one occasion, I said that I hoped Celtic won the league that season because that would help us qualify for Europe. It seemed logical. And factually correct. However, no matter how right I might have been to think it . . . I realized quickly that saying it was a mistake. Another incident to add to that list of mistakes is the time during my first season there when I said that it did not matter losing to Celtic as long as we won the league! Oops. Rangers fans, to a man and a woman, did not see it that way.

I am sure there were a lot who did not fancy me as manager. Probably the traditionalists. I had no history with the club, and plenty saw me as a big-time Charlie. There were ex-players who were bitter or maybe just jealous. When we were in Mexico at the 1986 World Cup and I was captain of Scotland, I was invited to have a drink one night with the coaches, and there was one of them – who maybe had enjoyed a tipple too many – who I felt was a bit jealous of my appointment. And, of course, I was a virgin as a manager.

I saw it another way. This was a club in the doldrums, and they should have welcomed anyone – from outer space if necessary – who could put some wind back in its sails. But I made one genius move when I brought John Greig – a fellow son of Edinburgh – back to the club. Greigy, like me, had gone straight from dressing room to manager's office, although in my time he did not have a job title. I brought him back just to be about the place. Just as a club legend. In fact, it was me who nicknamed him 'Ledge'. And you can genuinely file John Greig as a 24-carat example of the breed.

I remember him asking me what I wanted from him. I told him he had been named the club's greatest-ever player and was for sure its greatest-ever servant. I told him to do what he wanted, go where he fancied – including the dressing rooms on match days – at any time. Just be about the stadium. I wanted him to be a reminder of what this club stood for.

John just lit the place up and I always listened to him. He is a solid citizen, and I am proud to call him a friend. And, of course, he was captain of the club on those nights in my boyhood when my brother took me to the games, so it was quite special for me to have him around. I suppose Walter would have been there too . . .

So, anyway, after that nightmare defeat at Easter Road, we were off and running. Though it turned out to be a winning run of one . . . We beat Falkirk 1–0 at Ibrox, then lost the next week to a still-tasty Dundee United, before we got a 4–1 win over Stenhousemuir in the Skol League Cup. And then our league form clicked into gear. We beat Hamilton, Celtic, Motherwell and Clydebank, before losing to Dundee and then beating Aberdeen at Ibrox. I got a goal in that one.

Off the pitch that season, I was also signing serial winners. Men of real character. Jimmy Nicholl was a big-time Rangers fan who had started his football life at Manchester United, and had also been at Rangers earlier in his career, under Jock Wallace. He was a top guy and an experienced professional and Northern Ireland World Cup player who you would want in the trenches with you. He knew the score: you would not have to tell him, 'You're having a stinker, son.' Jimmy was proper old-school.

There was Graham Roberts too. I had played against him when he was at Spurs. He was no-nonsense but he could play. He fitted the criteria in an era when refereeing was different and opponents of Rangers didn't say to you: 'Let's have a jolly game of football today.' Robbo would say: 'You want a war? No problem, bring it on.' And then football would break out after he had settled things down.

But players had to go too. I decided to let Derek Johnstone, who had been an international teammate, leave the building. To be honest, despite his big personality his attitude was less professional than I would have wanted. He enjoyed his social life a bit too much and it was a bit like trying to teach an old dog new tricks. I needed everybody to buy into what I was trying to do. To be fair to him, he took it well. He knew it was coming.

And it was after that that I realized I had inherited a diamond. Davie Cooper, alongside Matt Le Tissier, Tugay and John Barnes, was one of the most talented players in terms of touch and dribbling ability that I have ever played with or managed. He was a Scotland teammate before I became his manager and he was with us in Mexico, but it was only when I saw him daily at Rangers that I understood how good he was. I do not know how he did the things he did, he had unbelievable ability. Had he had a different head on – he was such a home-loving boy who did not even drive – and had he had a different attitude, he could have become the greatest Scottish player ever. He was just blessed with talent, but he was a different kind of individual. He liked to keep his own counsel but could leave you dead with a killer line. I never heard one bad story about him.

Coop had been signed from Clydebank by Jock Wallace for £100,000 and had extended his contract before I arrived. I watched him play and listened to him. He just wanted to live a simple life and that is fair enough. But had he gone and embraced a different culture – perhaps with a move to Italy – he could have been anything. He was that good. He had a wand of a left foot and ice-cold blood running through his veins; he was a glorious striker of a football. There was, for instance, the sensational goal he made against Tampereen Ilves in Europe that first season. It began with as fine a solo run as you will ever see before he set it up for Robert Fleck.

I should never have let Coop go to Motherwell when I eventually did, in 1989 – there he became a cult hero all over again and a Scottish Cup winner – but by then I had signed Mark Walters and Trevor Steven, and I was well covered for wide men. He wanted to go because he wanted to be guaranteed a starting place every week and I could not agree to that. I told him he was still a big player for me and how, in tight games, he was the one with a key to unlock defences. But I did understand his point of view.

I loved him as a player, a World Cup teammate, and a pal. He had a unique talent. He was one cool dude. Motherwell paid us £50,000 and got themselves the biggest bargain in their history. I'll never forget his penalty in the 1986 Skol League Cup final against Celtic, which we won 2–1, with the other goal from Ian Durrant. Though in terms of pressure – and Hampden that day was threatening to blow the lid – it is dwarfed by the one he stuck away at Ninian Park in September 1985, the night Jock Stein died.

It was a World Cup qualifying game in which we needed a draw against Wales to proceed to a play-off against Australia. I was suspended and so out of the team. However, Big Jock insisted I travel from Italy to be at the game. So I was there when all hell broke loose at half-time after Mr Stein discovered that goalkeeper Jim Leighton wore contact lenses. Scotland were trailing 1–0 and Stein replaced Leighton with Alan Rough, a goalkeeper who could not spell 'panic', before we went in search of the equalizer. Then the manager brought on Coop. Little did we know on that tragic night that it would be Jock Stein's last moment of tactical genius.

It was nerve-wracking. And I would have loved to tell you what it was like to watch live. But I could not take it. So I went to the bar at Ninian Park. To my utter astonishment, in an otherwise deserted place I encountered

SFA chief Ernie Walker, who asked me what I was doing there. I asked him the same question and told him I could not stand the pressure of the game. 'Neither could I,' he said, and asked me what I wanted to drink. 'What's that you're drinking?' I asked, and he said: 'Scotch.' I had never drunk whisky before that night, nor have I drunk it since, but I said, 'I'll have what you're having,' and I swallowed it.

Coop scored the equalizing penalty, and we were on our way to Mexico . . . once we'd picked our way past Australia. Little did I know then that just a few months later I would be his boss. He was wonderful in every way.

Coop's death at the age of just thirty-nine was premature and tragic. He was still playing. It was a cruel and ridiculous loss. I remember at his funeral a youngish guy having a right go at me because I had let Coop leave Rangers. I was upset because he did not understand the full story. But those were the emotions Coop brought out in people, and I know now how wrong I was to sell him.

Stein and Cooper – the central figures on that night of heaven-turned-hell in Cardiff – both gone. Geniuses.

Big Jock died of a heart attack in the treatment room after the match, and I was in there amid the insanity of it. There were American-bar-style swing doors between the corridor and the treatment room where Jock was being treated by Stewart Hillis, the SFA doctor, who was a heart specialist. People were rushing about and the Big Man had his head tilted as he was being fed oxygen. I thought he was staring at me, but the horrific truth is that he was probably already dead.

It was devastating. It haunts me to this day. I still sit wide-eyed and think of what was thrown into our lives that night. He was one of the most influential figures world football – never mind the Scottish game – has ever known. Stein's achievements become even more remarkable as time goes by. In 1967 he made Celtic the first non-Latin European Cup winners, with a group of players born within thirty miles of Glasgow. Three years later he took them to another final. That all underlines the stature of the man.

And then he took Scotland to the 1982 World Cup finals in Spain, where I inherited the captaincy from Danny McGrain. I found Stein to be a wise old fox. He liked me – or he certainly acted that way – and I was horrified at the way events unfolded that night in Wales. Outside the stadium the euphoric Scottish fans were chanting his name and waiting for us to leave, not knowing – in the days before mobile phones and social media – what had happened. It was so sad. He was just sixty-two. I'll never forget what I learned from him.

Late in his life, I became friendly with the greatest football writer of all time, Hugh McIlvanney. Over lunch at the Savoy Hotel, I asked him to imagine a scenario in which he was sitting with Matt Busby, Bill Shankly, Don Revie, Brian Clough, Alex Ferguson and Jock Stein. Who did he think they would all be listening to. Who would be the dominant voice? Without hesitation, he said: 'Oh, Jock.'

Meanwhile, some players, like Graham Roberts (despite events later, which we will come to), made my life easy. These were the guys who trained properly and were part of a self-run dressing room. At Liverpool, by the time the manager entered the changing room at half-time, players would already be pointing the finger at one another and shouting, not waiting for the boss and coaching staff to produce answers. That is what I wanted at Ibrox. I never get fed up talking about the importance of having good senior pros at your club. As a manager, you have so little time to get your message across – four days a week, two hours a day – and you are working with twenty-five players. How much individual time can you give to them? This is where you need good senior pros, advising and demanding that the others do things the right way, to make sure you are successful.

Derek Ferguson and Ian Durrant benefitted from being beside some of the senior players we had at that time. Durrant was a special talent and I thought to myself that we would do well to keep him. The giants of the European game, I figured, would be knocking on our door once they'd heard about him. On top of being a talented player, he had a personality that made him a lovable rascal. But he knew how to rile me. We fell out at one point, and he asked for a transfer. He recalls that I picked up the *Rothmans Football Yearbook* – a thick tome that listed just about every football club in the world – and threw it at him, telling him to 'fucking pick one'.

Ian was box-to-box and he was fearless. He had more energy than any human being should have. The injury he suffered at Pittodrie, after finding himself on the wrong end of a horrific tackle, was a tragedy.

Derek Ferguson was capable of so much more than he achieved. But the problem, as I saw it, was that he just would not listen. I wondered about him away from Ibrox. He would leave on a Saturday and it would seem he was fine, then he'd come in on a Monday with a hamstring injury, triggered while playing five-a-side on a Sunday somewhere with his mates. Sometimes young lads need to move away from their neighbourhood and live a proper footballer's life. My mum never showed any resistance to me getting out of Edinburgh and heading to Spurs. She knew something.

So as these players came in, my first season was being shaped, but the support still didn't agree with my comment from the previous season about the desirability of Celtic winning the league. Whisper it, but Celtic's triumph over St Mirren on that dramatic last day of 1985–86, while Hearts stumbled against Dundee at Dens Park, opened the door to qualification for Europe and a jaunt around the continent in the UEFA Cup. We secured our place in our own final league fixture of the season, when – with me in the technical area for the first time – we defeated Motherwell 2–0, with goals from Ally McCoist and big Davie McPherson. But a lot of our fans were not that practical and could not countenance our great rivals as champions, no matter the compensation.

I had to learn that!

In any case, it brought my first taste of European football as a manager and we did OK. We beat Tampereen Ilves 4–0 at Ibrox, before stumbling a little but not fatally, losing the second leg 2–0 in Finland in front of our smallest crowd of the season, just 2,109. We then had a two-leg win over Boavista of Portugal, before going out on the away goals rule to Borussia Mönchengladbach of Germany. And rather unjustly at that. We drew 1–1 at Ibrox – Durrant scored in front of 43,000 – so needed a goal in Mönchengladbach to have any chance of progress.

I picked myself that night and we played well, but the odds were stacked against us and we finished with nine men. First Stu Munro was red-carded for retaliation while lying on the grass after he was kicked by André

Winkhold. Then Davie Cooper was sent off for asking the referee – Alexis Ponnet – if he was actually allowed to book any of the German players, following some shocking tackles on our players, Davie in particular. Despite the orderings off, I announced there would be no internal fines. That reflects how I felt.

But we had other fish to fry. What mattered most was the home front. The domestic championship is always your number one priority. And Rangers' last taste of it was fading into history. Just as well our priority was not the Scottish Cup. We went out of that in the first round, against Hamilton Accies, who would be relegated that season, and at Ibrox. It was just one of those days that happen in football, plus their goalkeeper, Dave McKellar, had the game of his life. I remember being calm about the whole matter, something that may shock some people, but football can throw up curious scorelines. The headline writers had a field day with our loss, but when you play a game with a bouncing ball then anything can happen, and I know, because I was on the park that day. The truth was that we had been on fire, a fact best illustrated by the statistic that during the game Chris Woods chalked up his 1,196th minute without losing a goal, before Adrian Sprott got one past him.

In any case, it served as a reality check. Although it did put the brakes on any hope of winning the treble, where hope was springing eternal given we had already won the Skol League Cup. After beating Stenhousemuir we'd knocked out lowly East Fife on penalties following a 0–0 draw – that was in an era when lower-division pitches were a joke. The quarter-finals saw a 3–1 win at Ibrox over Dundee, before we beat their neighbours – the still-quality Dundee United – in the semi-final.

And so I got my first trip to Hampden as a manager in a final. Of course, it had to be Celtic. Winning League Cup finals will not keep you in your job at Ibrox but beating Celtic always helps. And we did that thanks to goals from Ian Durrant and Coop, with Brian McClair scoring for them.

I was injured and Derek Ferguson played in my role and was brilliant. It was a fiery game with ten bookings. But it was Durrant who won the sponsor's prize – Concorde flights for two – for scoring the opening goal. I can't believe I didn't nick them from him! When did he think I was going to let him off to enjoy those? After that opening goal, we got a penalty when Terry Butcher – of all people – was floored by Roy Aitken. Coop took care of what happened next, as he always did, before the bedlam ensued . . . Mo Johnston – who was then a Celtic player and who had no idea of the twist his life was going to take – was sent off, and so too was Tony Shepherd, before referee David Syme, who curiously thought that Shepherd had thrown a coin at him, changed his mind and allowed him to stay on the park. Oh, and Celtic manager Davie Hay – a very dear friend and one of the really good guys – was on the pitch arguing with the officials.

Old Firm games, for the avoidance of any doubts, are not children's parties.

If I was pondering whether life was ever again going to be the same, then this was confirmation that I had moved into madhouse central . . . and I have to say I was loving it. Mind you, there were a couple of things that needed addressing. There was a league championship to be won. And a bomb to let off under a signing policy that had been in place at Rangers since day one and that had put us in the position of trying to win regattas while dragging an anchor.

The peace and quiet and tranquil beauty of Nervi were all beginning to seem very far away indeed.

4

A Man Wants to Kiss My Feet

So the season proved a mixture of trying to win the crown and dealing with the team clown.

Ally McCoist, in another life, could have been a stand-up comedian. But he used to drive me crazy. Coisty had spent his childhood in East Kilbride and so was pretty much a local lad. He was brought up as a Rangers fan, despite starting his career with St Johnstone and Sunderland. Ibrox was always going to be his ultimate destination.

As a player, he had a wonderful sixth sense that allowed him to be in the right place at the right time. He did not always fancy running the channels and he certainly was not the workhorse that Mo Johnston later proved to be. But McCoist was a rascal who did not always apply himself to the ways of a reliable professional. For example, Mark Hateley, who later joined the club, had honed his football education in Italy and knew the required life-style. His father Tony had played at the highest level and had clearly taught his son how to apply himself to the game. You didn't find Hateley in kebab shops late at night. I could not say the same about your man McCoist. Ally, like the rest of us when we have had a drink, thought he was invisible. But this was Rangers and everyone knew everyone's business, so my phone was always ringing off its hook with people telling me where my players were. And often it was where they should not have been.

In that first season, in the early hours of 5 December 1986, McCoist and Ian Durrant were charged with breach of the peace and assault after an incident with an eighteen-year-old in a chip shop in East Kilbride. Durrant was on crutches and Coisty was only protecting his pal against some guy who turned on him. Ted McMinn, another party animal, was out with them too. When it went to court, the charges against Ian were thrown out but Ally was convicted of minor assault and fined £150.

Months later, on the bus back from Pittodrie, after we had won the title, I called them down the front and told them I was fining them £1,500 each for the business in the chippy. Apart from anything else they had been out forty-eight hours before a game. But I also told them that if they behaved for the next six months, they would get it back. And they did.

Durrant had another situation a couple of years later, after he had suffered that terrible injury at Pittodrie. This time he was with Derek Ferguson, in a kebab shop near the stadium, and someone suggested that Neil Simpson should have broken his other leg too. That went to court, but this time Ian was handed a not proven verdict.

Alistair, meanwhile, thought he could get away with a trip down to the horse racing at Cheltenham and that I would not find out. Was he mad? I tried to tell him that travelling all that way and back in twenty-four hours, taking into account the slight possibility that he might have had a sherbet or two, was not good for a professional athlete's body. And I made him publicly apologize to his teammates and the support. I also dropped him from the team for the next game.

If I constantly threatened him, it was only to try to get the best out of him. But there were other times I turned a blind eye, because he did have a magic about him. His remarkable goalscoring record was nothing to do with luck, it was his sense of the game that was top-class. That was his gift. There were games in which we did not play well but we won thanks to Ally's ability to put the ball in the net.

He was a natural goalscorer. And he gave so much to our dressing room. I was aware that, as the manager, I should not overstay my welcome there; I had to let the boys get on with it. But I will be honest, McCoist's chat had me hanging around longer than I had intended, so I could just listen in.

The football dressing room is not for the easily offended. It is a hard school. And short on political correctness. Way short! The atmosphere can be ferocious, and indeed cruel, but you sink or swim. And the higher you go in the game, the harder the banter. If you are easily offended, it's probably not a suitable habitat for you.

McCoist had the worst timekeeping of anyone I have ever known, matched only by his unreliability, which continues until this day. He pushed the boundaries, but mostly he got away with it because of his personality. He was king of the dressing room. But also he knew where the back of the net was. Alistair Murdoch McCoist scored thirty-four goals for us that title-winning season and was a key component of our all-conquering championship side.

Once we cemented Chris Woods in our team, I was confident we could do this title-winning thing and set Rangers purring again. Not that it was straightforward. On 22 November we lost 1–0 to Aberdeen at Pittodrie, with Dave McPherson red-carded. That left us eight points behind leaders Celtic.

But then we clicked. We did not lose a league game again until Celtic beat us 3–1 at Celtic Park in the spring, 4 April to be exact. We beat Hearts, St Mirren, Hibs, Falkirk, Hamilton, Dundee United, Celtic, Motherwell, Clydebank, Hamilton, Aberdeen, Hearts, St Mirren, and then drew with Hibs, before getting all three points against

Falkirk, Hamilton, Dundee, Dundee United and Motherwell. And after that defeat to Celtic we did not lose in the title race again. We romped home from there.

I particularly enjoyed my first taste of a Ne'erday derby against our oldest rivals, when we beat them 2–0 with goals from Robert Fleck and McCoist. I played very well that day. We were miles better than the scoreline suggests and I knew that Celtic would not be able to handle the pressure we were putting on them. It was a massive win.

There were a lot of key games. When we beat Hamilton Accies on 17 January, we went to the top of the league; the first time we had been there at that point of the season in nine years. Albeit we blew it against them in the Scottish Cup two weeks later! One postscript to this . . . we got back on the horse, Hamilton got relegated.

After we lost to Hamilton in the cup, we played Hearts, who had been championship runners-up the previous season, only missing out on the last day, so they were a good team. The game was at Tynecastle, a ground that had become their fortress. And they were managed by a couple of Rangers heroes – members of the team that won the European Cup Winners' Cup in 1972 – Alex MacDonald and Sandy Jardine. They had some talented players, like Craig Levein, Gary Mackay and John Robertson. When we beat them 5–2 – I even got a goal – I knew we were on our way. Confidence is a wonderful thing to have, and I have been blessed to have had it all my life.

We were cruising, and among the victories was a win over a Dundee United side who were at the time on their way to the UEFA Cup final. This run included the elimination of Barcelona. If that is not proof enough, here's how good United were back in the day. They have played Barça four times and have a 100 per cent record against one of the world's genuinely great football clubs. They were an extraordinarily formidable team that year. And Scottish football was clearly on a high.

By this point in the season we were defensively tight and we had stopped conceding goals. Well, with Butcher and Woods in your gang, you would, wouldn't you? As we edged towards the climax, I remember thinking that we were good but that we could be better. That was the Liverpool attitude kicking in . . . never happy, always looking for us to improve. I wanted to instil that ruthlessness I had learned from Bob Paisley, Joe Fagan, Ronnie Moran and Jack Charlton. And Jock Stein, of course.

In the end, everything came down to the events of 2 May 1987.

No matter what Celtic were doing against Falkirk at Parkhead, we would be champions for the first time in nine years if we could draw in our penultimate game of the season, against Aberdeen at Pittodrie. It had been a long time since Rangers had stood on this threshold. The expectation levels and delight of our supporters were through the roof. Not that we were taking anything for granted. Aberdeen had skilful players, like my international teammates Jim Leighton, Alex McLeish, Willie Miller and David Robertson. David would later go on to play for Rangers. Jim Bett too. I wanted to sign him and tried hard, but he was too nice a guy for a Mexican stand-off with Alex Ferguson and the board in those pre-Bosman days. So it never happened.

We knew it was going to be a challenge, but a draw would put us two points ahead in the days of two points for a win, with a vastly superior goal difference. Until then, we had conceded only twenty-two goals in forty-two league matches. That is some case for the defence. Our fans were going crazy for the season's climax. The capacity of Pittodrie back then was 24,000 and Rangers fans could have filled that four times over. Officially, our club were given 5,000 tickets for the Beach End. But the black market was doing some business.

The welcome that Rangers got at Pittodrie was up there with what we got at Parkhead, and the bitterness surprised me. The growth of that animosity had not been helped, I think, by Alex Ferguson and the time he had spent persuading his northeastern supporters that the west of Scotland had it in for them . . . ironic coming from a man born in Govan. I think Alex Ferguson stoked that kind of thing, because he later used the 'no one likes us' mentality at Manchester United. In any case, the Aberdeen fans did not like the idea of Rangers being reborn and taking over again. As for Fergie, I have always had a fabulous relationship with him and understand that what happened back then is all part of the game. He has been very generous with his time in helping me raise funds with my charity, DEBRA, of which I am vice president.

And even back then I think I understood that he was just playing the game and battling for his fans. If anything, that extra edge added to our swagger. We knew how sweet it would be to win it there.

Unfortunately, my championship season was to end the way it began . . . with another red card. With just over half an hour gone, I was sent off for a tackle around the halfway line on Brian Irvine, who made the most of it by staying down. I certainly did not properly catch him, and it might have been a yellow at worst. But the referee John Duncan seemed to be intimidated by the reaction of the Aberdeen crowd, as well as by their bench and their players, who were baying for my blood, which always was the case when I was playing for Rangers in Scotland. It seemed to me that they definitely swayed Duncan, who I felt should have been stronger. And so I got my marching orders.

My tackle on Irvine was never a sending off but I

1. Let the sign do the talking. I don my Rangers working gear for the first time.

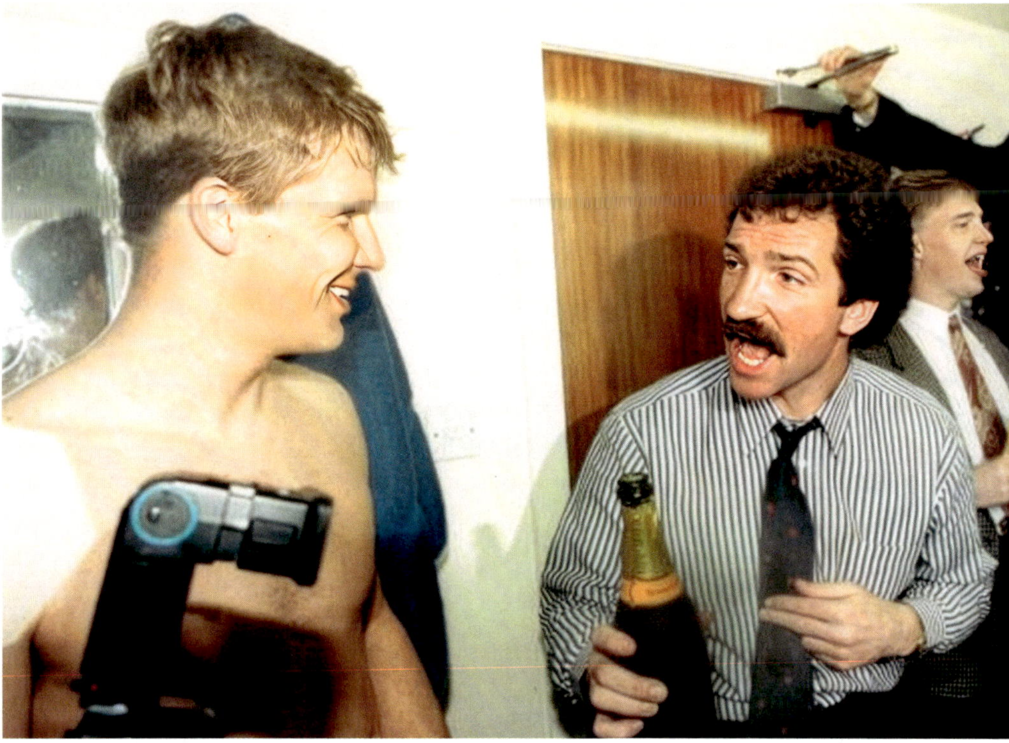

2. Our first major signing was Chris Woods who triggered us poaching from the England team. I promised him the champagne lifestyle and we didn't let him down.

3. Two brilliant men with the cars to match. Walter Smith and David Holmes at the gates to blue heaven.

4. The man behind the desk. I get used to the other side of the job in my manager's office at Ibrox.

5. Two of the best signings I made and again we reverse the north–south traffic. Terry Butcher and Graham Roberts show off the double.

6. (*Above*) Davie Cooper in full flow as I look on approvingly. I should never have let him go.

7. (*Left*) This time I got the genius to sign a new deal.

8. (*Right*) Start them young. Me coming to Ibrox hopefully triggered another generation of Rangers supporters.

9. (*Below*) A moment of reflection for me and Doc Donald Cruickshank at Il Ciocco at pre-season. He was a diamond of a man.

10. At this time I thought I was at Rangers for the long stretch. Pre season at Il Ciocco.

11. There was a lot of thinking to be done about where Rangers go next.

12. Me with my training coach and great buddy Phil Boersma. He was a massive hit with the players and a fabulous friend.

13. Me and Walter in the boot room. He was an absolute delight of a human being. My right-hand man.

14. Some key figures in the Rangers revolution. Beside me Lawrence Marlborough – who owned the club – and vice chairman Jack Gillespie. In front are David Murray and David Holmes who were both to become chairmen.

15. What a debut at Easter Road. But my tackle on George McCluskey wasn't where the trouble all started.

16. It wasn't me, ref. I plead my innocence in a European tie against Boavista. The opposition doesn't look that convinced.

was still angry with myself. Despite people saying things to the contrary, I was not a serial offender. My career statistics confirm that I was sent off once in England, and twice in Italy – both times by the same official. It was not a regular occurrence for me.

After I was shown the red, I headed straight for the tunnel, which at Pittodrie is in the corner, while all hell broke loose on the pitch. I do not remember looking at our bench and Walter certainly knew not to say anything to me. I was not allowed to return to the technical area and so watched from the tunnel as events unfolded. What I saw next will never leave me. Terry Butcher scored before Brian Irvine equalized, but it did not matter because we knew a draw would be enough.

Celtic lost 2–1 to Falkirk that day. Their party was over. But ours was just beginning.

There was one incident after the full-time whistle that has stuck with me all these years. Mayhem had ensued and the Rangers fans were on the pitch. Those of our supporters who did not get tickets and had waited outside stormed in through the newly opened exit gates. The goalposts were torn down, in a way reminiscent of the aftermath of Scotland's victory at Wembley ten years earlier. It was a little scary at times. Players lost jerseys and boots. Ally McCoist lost the gold chain round his neck . . . although I think it was later returned by a guilt-ridden fan. But then this one bloke, a fully grown man in his fifties, came up to me and asked me ever so politely if he could kiss my feet. I had never heard nor seen the like before, and haven't since. But it was the one moment when I suddenly got what it meant to be a Rangers supporter. And what the club did for them.

The real love and passion these people had and have for this football club. It was a way of life for them. And I got it now. There were tears of gratitude in the eyes of the fans. Their reactions were awe-inspiring. These people lived for Glasgow Rangers and suddenly their world was a better place. In that moment I realized I had done the right thing coming to Ibrox.

I had never seen passion like that for a club before. Obviously, the fact that we had not won the league for a decade had something to do with it. Not even at Liverpool, where we won three European Cups and five titles in seven seasons, did I witness anything like this. You see what it means to lose or win an Old Firm game, and when you are the manager you realize the incredible level of responsibility you have been given. That is what kept me awake at night. But in this moment, though, there was also blessed relief.

So we had a party to get started, but nothing to start it with, it seemed. I had banned champagne, and party hats and t-shirts that anticipated us winning the title, on the bus to Pittodrie. I had not wanted to tempt fate. A mantra honed at Liverpool. I cannot recall if Aberdeen gave us a couple of cases of bubbly or we got some from elsewhere, but eventually we made it out of their stadium, through the celebrating fans and on to the bus that would speed us back to Glasgow. Once the coach was on its way, the party was off and running, and everyone, it seemed, wanted to join in. I remember one police officer waving us through the red traffic lights on the outskirts of Aberdeen and clenching his fist in celebration to the packed coach.

Not everyone in the northeast despised us after all. In fact, all the way south we were waved on our way by friendly officers. A few Rangers fans must have volunteered for shifts that day. The truth is that the love of Rangers is not restricted to Glasgow and the west. A love of the club stretches the length and breadth of the country. We made it back to Ibrox to be welcomed by the players' wives and girlfriends and an ocean of flag-waving fans. For once, I told the players to do what they wanted. Just this once!

We were presented with the championship trophy the following week, in our final game of the season, against St Mirren at Ibrox. The authorities wanted a pre-match ceremony, but I insisted on the trophy being handed over *after* the match. I did not want the players to be anything other than 100 per cent concentrated. Again, that was the state of mind I'd learned at Liverpool.

We were serial winners at Anfield but never celebrated until the job was done, and then only briefly before moving on to the next campaign. At the start of the season after a trophy was won, Ronnie Moran would come into the dressing room with an old cardboard box and throw it on the massage table. He would say, 'There's some medals in there, if you played enough games and you think you deserve one, take one,' and then walk out the door. But six or seven seconds later he would stick his head back in to see if anyone had made a move. We were all frightened to be the first, even me and Kenny Dalglish! It was all aimed at not letting any of us get too carried away with ourselves. Ronnie was the biggest influence on my career. He was a big part of my football education. 'You're good,' he would say to us, 'but not as good as we had in the past.' I responded to his hardness. He had a way about him that was tough but endearing. If we won something, the celebrations were all over within twenty-four hours and we were off in pursuit of something else. He wanted us back on the horse quickly.

I took that attitude to Rangers, and the longer I was there the less I had to shout and be angry, because I had talented players who got it. So after we won that first championship, four days from my thirty-fourth birthday, for me it was time to reflect. As I've already mentioned, I think my overriding emotion was relief. And belief that we could go again. We had become a solid group of guys. But even as I packed to head back to Majorca for a much-needed holiday, I understood that there was plotting for the days ahead to be done: we were on a mission and there was no time to stand still. The following season, 1987–88, would be Celtic's centenary, and we knew the stakes would be upped.

We had qualified for the European Cup which, while not the Champions League now, was far more prestigious than the UEFA Cup, certainly significant enough to tempt big-name players from north and south of the border. And while we had a great team, we still had to crack this ancient signing policy. Though we were getting closer. Ray Houghton, who had been at Oxford United but was Glasgow-born, originally considered coming to Rangers, before changing his mind and signing for Liverpool. I can understand that, because as soon as there were even rumours about the move he started receiving threats, including a bullet in the post. And John Collins at Hibs was a player I greatly admired. But that clearly did not happen either.

Religious issues apart, in those days no player ever said 'no' to Rangers, even if most clubs had an issue about selling to us. I was lucky I had David Holmes as my chairman, because he was a visionary for the club. Within days of the title being wrapped up, he unveiled a credit card scheme that up to 10,000 supporters could join by paying £180 per head. This would guarantee Rangers £1.6 million before the next season even got under way. The plan, which cost £15 a month, was launched in an effective effort to cut down queues for tickets at home games. David envisaged a time when full computerization would be in operation, allowing fans with a plastic card to just tap in at the gate. It might seem very 'so what?' now, because it has become the norm, but back then it was groundbreaking. He announced plans to build a new office block at the stadium behind the Govan – now the Sandy Jardine – stand, and all the profits generated from selling other assets owned by the club would be ploughed back into the club. All the administrative staff would be housed in one place.

David and his wonderful wife Betty – who sadly recently passed away – were the heart and soul of Rangers at the time. I loved and appreciated their support, but they also took the time to engage with the fans. David and Betty would attend supporters' functions and listen to what the people there had to say. He was the single biggest reason the club engaged with the fans.

All of that made my life so much easier. Given this was my first managerial role, David was all I knew, so I assumed all clubs were run like this. I was in for a real shock in the future!

The people at the club were not all like that, though. Two of the directors, Hugh Adam and Freddie Fletcher, whom I'd had very little interaction with, privately wrote to owner Lawrence Marlborough, who was still living in Nevada, expressing their tradition-rooted concerns about the way David and I were running the club. Marlborough promptly read their letters, popped them back in an envelope and returned them across the Atlantic to David, telling him to do what he saw fit. The chairman at once showed them to me!

David Holmes ran everything except football matters, which he left to me. That was perfect. You cannot run football clubs by committee. It must be autocratic. What David did was lay the foundations for the nine championships in a row that Rangers eventually won. His contribution to the club should never be forgotten; he was a godsend to Glasgow Rangers. What I did on my end was to try and pass on to the players what I had learned at Liverpool and in Italy: how to train, live and behave.

I was also taught at Anfield to play things down, to be humble and not to rile your opposition. I tried to exemplify and teach those virtues in my first season at Ibrox. But being humble did not work with Rangers and so I had a Jim Carrey in *The Mask* moment. Except I took mine off when it dawned on me that there was no goodwill towards us. I thought to myself, 'OK, if that's the way you want it,' and I released the real Graeme Souness.

'No one likes us, we don't care.' That is what they sing at Ibrox. I became the man the media and others painted me to be. We were realizing very quickly that around the country there were only a few people, members of the media, or clubs outside Govan who had any time or respect for us. The majority were green with envy about what was happening at Ibrox.

I do recall one exception. East Fife had a chairman called Jim Baxter – not that one – who was an absolute gentleman and showed genuine appreciation of what we were trying to do. He and his lady wife were a charming couple. He was a lovely bloke who passed on a while back, but his warmth always stuck with me.

In any case, in the summer of '87 the real ebullient, snarling, tell-them-straight Souness emerged into the light. Most of Scottish football could go forth and multiply. Celtic had replaced Davie Hay with Billy McNeill, and we knew a big challenge was coming, and not only did I have no time for people hating us, but it lit a fire under me to improve the team even more.

So we bought the best player I ever signed, though it came about a year later than we intended because of the way Scottish clubs felt about Rangers. The previous season, Jim McLean at Dundee United – who seemed to have a particular issue with us – had refused at any price to sell Richard Gough to me. Another perfect example of 'anyone but Rangers'. They did not seem to realize that we would get there somewhere down the road. He went to Spurs for a season and played in the FA Cup final, which they lost 3–2 to Coventry, but in the wake of that we paid my old club £1.6 million for him (arguably the money rustled up by David's credit card scheme). Let me tell you, though, he was well worth the wait. The fee was a bargain. He was quality on and off the pitch, an outstanding professional in every way. Richard was a proper warrior. An unbelievable athlete. You never had to wonder if he was living properly. He was a fitness fanatic. His attitude was always 100 per cent, and as well as being a wonderful defender he was a real threat up front in dead-ball situations. When we played small-sided games at training, I always tried to get on his side because even in these matches he was all elbows and knees. He was a diamond and just as hard. So it's no surprise that Gough went on to become the club's most decorated captain. He won eighteen major trophies, including nine successive league titles, three Scottish Cups and six League Cups in 427 appearances. Incidentally, I am hoping his wife at the time does not read this. I seem to remember I promised to buy her a fur coat if he came back to Scotland.

Players came and players went as we tried to improve the squad, including my old mate from Italy, Trevor Francis, who came in from Atalanta. He was at the veteran stage and I told him he would not be playing every week, but he was a great professional and character and another one the young players could look up to and learn from. Meanwhile, I could feel the referee looking at his watch in terms of my own playing career. I had something to give yet, but as I went into the summer of '87, I wondered how much juice was left in the tank. The player-manager combination was a tough shift. There were not too many around and I was beginning to understand why! I had to be a player in the morning at training, then a manager in the afternoon, and then a player or manager again in the evening – depending on whether or not we had a game. If we did not have a match, then Walter and I would often pop off down to England to watch potential Rangers players performing somewhere. It was a gruelling routine.

I missed a few days at the start of the 1987–88 season because of an old injury, so I had a Dutch physio move in with me at my home in Edinburgh and come to Ibrox daily to address the issues in my calves. In fact, I used to lie on my kitchen worktop – because it was the right height – to allow him proper access to my calf muscles with his elbows. A suitable place, because something was cooking with my own career, and at Ibrox, and we were about to find out whether retaining a championship was more difficult than winning it.

There was a league title to defend, a centenary celebration to fend off and a European Cup to be attacked. We had come a long way in a brief time, but then Rangers have an old song about the road being broad or narrow. However, with the remarkable support there was no distance that could not be travelled. That is how we felt as we thundered into my second season in charge.

But Scottish football is, of course, the greatest soap opera and our tale was just starting to unfold.

Though the headlines were getting bigger, Lawrence Marlborough sounded a note of caution. While on a rare transatlantic visit to Ibrox, to share in the title celebrations on the last day of the season, he warned: 'We are actually a bit ahead in our planning, but we won't kid ourselves that there won't be setbacks in the future.'

There spoke a wise man . . .

5

Though the Pitch Be Broad or Narrow . . .

Jock Stein used to say, 'Don't go looking for trouble as a football manager, it will find you,' and throughout my career, I sure have had my share of confrontations.

I can remember my mother shaking her head in disbelief and telling me when I was a wee boy that 'There's never a dull moment when you're around, son'.

In my time in Scotland, my relationship with the media was sometimes fractious, and I think in part that had to do with my education about the press on Merseyside. At Liverpool, we were instructed to engage as infrequently as we could, and that was a mantra that was passed down from generation to generation. We were told that, generally, they were not our friends.

So, by the time I'd arrived at Ibrox, I had had no media training – unlike players and coaches in the modern game.

It was not until years later, when I worked for newspapers, radio and television, that I started to learn about their business. In the eighties I was a complete novice and was flying on a wing and a prayer.

I was also entering a completely unfamiliar media environment. At Liverpool, Bob Paisley would have a chat about team news and that sort of stuff on a Friday with just one of the press pack, and then it would all be passed around. Bob did it on his terms and others followed. Alex Ferguson, in his later years with Manchester United, went to war with parts of the media, particularly the BBC. But back then, Glasgow was a whole new ball game. Fergie, when he was at Aberdeen, had already decided that the west of Scotland press were anti his northeastern club. That implied a degree of unity that didn't square with my experience. It seemed to me the entire media in our city was divided right down the middle in terms of being anti or pro Rangers or Celtic. And then there were a few who just had it in for us. I thought it was all small-minded and parochial. We even tried to diminish the outrageous headlines by putting a media company between me and the press. The idea was that I'd brief Alan Ferguson of Pro Scot, who would then speak to the papers on my behalf. It was a system that the press wouldn't accept, so that lasted about two weeks!

Sadly, on two occasions I was close to getting physical

with members of the press. Although I would have enjoyed it, I accepted that it would not have been the way for a Rangers manager to behave. It was a different time back then. At the age of thirty-four, I was super confident and ready for any challenge coming my way – I felt I could handle anything life could throw at me. If it had happened all over again at a different point in my life, I'm not sure whether I would have gone into it with the same ability or aggression. Had I got the job aged forty-three, would I have been brave enough to make the difficult decisions I did early in my managerial career? There is a swagger and self-confidence that come with youth that seem to dissipate as you age. I was fearless back then.

But it was not just journalists at whom I lashed out. In that second season, we crashed out of the Scottish Cup at East End Park against a Dunfermline side who had in goals – would you believe it? – former Hamilton man Dave McKellar, who had denied us a year earlier while performing for the Accies. He had returned to haunt us wearing another strip!

It was just his second game for them and we lost 2–0 – as well as John Brown to a red card. This Scottish Cup was becoming an elusive thing to win. Our thirteen-man squad that day had eleven international players, who had 348 caps between them. This was a game we should have won. You can see why I expected us to triumph. And yet it illustrates once again how much inferior players lift their game when they play Rangers.

Of course, you can slip up in any game, but I preached to my players that when you play for Glasgow Rangers every ninety minutes is a cup final for the opposition. I wanted to help them keep their instinct against even the smallest teams. However, it is a bouncing ball, and sometimes a big team loses to a small team.

For all that, I went nuts at the end of the game. In the East End Park visitors' dressing room was an old television set, which I am not sure even worked. In any case, in my rage I booted it and put my foot through the screen. If it did not work before, it sure was not going to work now.

I had a temper but mostly I controlled it. When you play at the top level the pressure is immense, and it multiplies a thousandfold when you are the manager. And at Glasgow Rangers it is as hot as it gets. As I've already said, this is a job where being second means failure. It is a job where you know that if you lose then it makes the lives of a whole community miserable. I think I got that there was a section of the support who lived for Rangers winning, and I felt for them when we did lose. I understood their angst.

So the Scottish Cup campaign was scuppered again, but we made a better fist of our assault on the European Cup, reaching the last eight. We started knowing that the further we got, the bigger the names would be. The best of the European game. We began our campaign with an away game against Dynamo Kyiv, formerly called Kiev Dynamo, and came away from what was still called the Soviet Union – now Ukraine – with a 1–0 defeat thanks to a penalty awarded when Oleksiy Mykhaylychenko went down in the box on the end of a tackle from Graham Roberts. The Austrian referee, Franz Wöhrer, pointed to the spot. Mykhaylychenko consequently scored. In years to come, Mykhaylychenko would sign for Rangers and become a fan favourite. He had a real talent. The game was played in front of a crowd of 100,000, of which there were fewer than 100 in the band of Rangers fans because of issues with visas.

Anyway, we returned to Ibrox for the second leg two weeks later and I knew we had a job on our hands against a fine team who made up the nucleus of the Soviet Union's side.

It was clearly going to be tough, but I came up with an idea. As is the UEFA rule, they trained on the Ibrox surface the night before the game, and having discussed it with Walter, we hatched a cunning plan.

I decided the best tactic was to narrow the pitch for the match itself, and make the ninety minutes as physical as possible, because we had players who enjoyed that part of the game. Dynamo Kyiv liked to deploy the full width of the playing surface and feed their left winger, Ivan Yaremchuk, and their superstar Oleh Blokhin.

In those days there were maximum and minimum dimensions, and as long as your pitch fell within those parameters you were OK. Crucially, you did not have to specify to anybody the pitch's exact length and width. So, on the match day, I instructed groundsman Davie Roxburgh to get to work and take in the touchlines as much as was legally allowed. I will never forget Dynamo coming out for their warm-up and having to run across the track, and then another twenty steps further than the night before just to cross the white line to get on the pitch. And I *was* watching. Although I was in the starting line-up, and therefore already in my playing kit, I had gone up to the directors' box to position myself out of sight so I could see their reaction.

Dynamo were a really good team, with better players than us, and they were furious about the shrinking pitch, but the plan worked perfectly and we won 2–0 with goals from Mark Falco and Ally McCoist.

Representatives from Dynamo complained to the UEFA observer immediately after the game and our groundsman had to measure the pitch in front of them to satisfy their furious demands. I returned to my perch in the directors' box to watch this, and I was praying Davie had not got it wrong. Luckily (though unsurprisingly) our man had got it spot on and we were in the clear, but the next season UEFA changed the rules and clubs had to register their pitch dimensions at the start of every season and then commit to not changing them. That was down to us. It is still the case today.

In the next round, we beat Górnik 3–1 at Ibrox – where we were 3–0 up at half-time – before drawing 1–1 in Poland. McCoist scored our penalty. By now we were in the quarters for just the fifth time in the history of the club and the opposition was the Romanian side Steaua Bucharest, a right good team peppered with real players, like the world-class Gheorghe Hagi, whose son Ianis eventually ended up playing for Glasgow Rangers. Steaua had won the tournament two years earlier.

I had a bit of previous with Romanians from my Liverpool days, in particular against Dinamo, the other team from Bucharest, who we faced in the 1984 European Cup semi-final. At Anfield, a player called Lică Movilă and I had tangled several times, so out of frustration I lashed out and, unfortunately for him, caught him with a punch that broke his jaw.

Having been there with Liverpool, I knew Rangers would have a challenging time in the first leg in Romania. We lost 2–0. Marius Lăcătuș had been part of Steaua's European Cup-winning team of 1986 and is still their all-time leading goalscorer in Europe. He was an exceptionally talented player, and also a master of the dark arts. As good as he was, Lăcătuş was extremely naughty in the first game, topping players and showing his studs at every opportunity, so I thought to myself: 'If I get half a chance in the second game, I am going to leave a bit on him.' Early in the match, the opportunity arose and I hit him with the most ridiculous challenge, about which I am embarrassed to this day! As I clattered the unfortunate, innocent victim – it turned out to be a chap called Iosif Rotariu – I looked up to see Lăcătuş standing hands on hips a few feet away, laughing his bollocks off. He knew exactly what had happened.

It was a case of mistaken identity, your honour. Looking back, I should have been arrested, never mind given a red card. Though I hadn't been hurt at all, I thought I was going to be sent off, so I went down holding my Achilles, looking for sympathy . . . which I got from the referee. And I actually stayed on the park. I should have received an Academy Award.

Richard Gough got a goal, and Ally McCoist tucked a penalty away, but despite winning on the night we were out on aggregate because Lăcătuş – of course – had scored an early opener.

The whole tie against Steaua threw up an unnecessary sideshow. In the first leg, McCoist, it seemed, had just come along for the ride, because he'd had some cartilage trimmed ten days earlier. But he asked if he could train with the squad on the eve of the game. After training, he told me there had been no reaction and that, against all odds, he felt good enough to play the following night.

McCoist playing led to a confrontation with a Scottish journalist who claimed I had kept the story from him and his colleagues and given it to the English press. The Scottish writers had missed the story because they had not come to the final training session, as they were all out for dinner. Or, more likely, on the piss. Again, an example of expecting plenty coming out of the club but showing little support for what we were achieving.

On the flight home straight after the game, the team had boarded and I was in the third-row at the window seat, beside Walter and coach Phil Boersma. As the press boarded, the individual concerned started to rant at me that I had kept the McCoist story from him and his Scottish colleagues while I fed it to the English contingent. He then moved several rows back up the plane. After that, my head was boiling and I clambered over Walter and Phil to get to him and explain that it was his love of alcohol and his non-appearance at training that had stopped him from getting the story. I was absolutely raging at him. But physical contact, there was none.

Meanwhile, we blew our effort to retain the championship, mainly because Terry Butcher broke his leg against Aberdeen in the sixth minute of a game at Ibrox in November, which ruled him out for the rest of the season. It had an enormous impact on us.

The squad was evolving dramatically. We signed John Brown from Dundee to replace Terry, although he was a genuine utility player. I had first come across Bomber when he played against us for Dundee and he was having a right go at me and coming back for more. Nothing fazed him, no matter how much I tried to rattle his cage. Not one iota. He had a fire in his eyes. At half-time I said to Walter: 'Who the fuck is that number 6?' He said: 'That's Bomber. He's a huge Rangers fan.' So I thought: 'We need to go get him.'

We paid Dundee £350,000 and he was brilliant. Bomber's dream game would have involved the referee blowing their whistle before leaving the pitch – it would then be a match of last man standing. He was and is a true blue. He is passionate and devoted to the Rangers cause, and I have never seen anyone who behaved like he did in the dressing room before games. But he did have one problem when it came to playing for Rangers. Bomber's excitement levels went stratospheric. He actually hyperventilated and had to breathe into a brown paper bag for fifteen minutes before kick-off to calm himself down. Seriously. He is some man.

And then there was the case of Mark Walters. I loved

his ability to dribble and excite fans, and I knew the Rangers support would love him. We signed him from Aston Villa for £500,000 on New Year's Eve 1987 and he went straight into the team for the Old Firm match. I knew Villa chairman Doug Ellis who, like me, had a place in Majorca, and we both agreed about Mark's talents. He was a reluctant seller, but they needed the money.

Mark was quick, brave and an all-round fabulous footballer. And a right good lad. But he did have his challenges in Scotland, where some opposing fans would racially abuse him. It was disgraceful and embarrassing that at some grounds bananas were thrown on to the pitch. It was beyond moronic and it made you wonder what century these idiots thought it was. What is the matter with some people? It was horrific.

In one game, he was so angry and upset he had tears in his eyes; he was being racially abused by the player he was up against. I told Mark to go show his antagonist how good he was . . . and he did. In the second half, he ripped his opponent apart with a dazzling display, embarrassing the full back in question. He humiliated him. I could name the player, but I would not even want to acknowledge him.

We moved Mark Falco, who we'd picked up that summer from Watford, to Queens Park Rangers after just a few short months, thereby turning a £250,000 profit – though Mark did not stay long, he scored ten goals in nineteen games, a valuable contribution. And I sold Robert Fleck to Norwich. I knew he would do well, but he was a victim of Rangers being in a hurry. Time is not your friend when you are manager of a football club, especially one like Rangers, and I could not wait for him to develop, but I am glad he had an illustrious career in England.

And then a player came in who went on to become a Rangers legend, taking part in every instalment of the nine in a row. Ian Ferguson had won the Scottish Cup the previous season with St Mirren but was a through-and-through Rangers fan, despite having been brought up in the shadow of Celtic Park. St Mirren adopted the traditional stance of Scottish clubs and did not want to sell to us, but we persuaded them with good money, and it helped how much he wanted to come to Ibrox.

Fergie was also the man who made me realize my playing days were numbered. I was always strong and comfortable in possession of the ball, but I recall how easily he brushed me off it on one occasion and it was the first indication to me that the clock was ticking.

There was a lot of thinking to be done. About myself . . . and my team. We retained the Skol League Cup, beating Stirling Albion and Dunfermline, thrashing a good Hearts team 4–1, then Motherwell, and drawing 3–3 in the final with Aberdeen, before winning on penalties.

But our efforts to retain the title flopped in Celtic's centenary season. In fact, we didn't even finish second. Hearts beat us to that by a couple of points. I had been sent off against Celtic at Parkhead in the first Old Firm game of the season, and after just five games the writing already seemed to be on the wall . . . three points from a possible ten. It was a nightmare start.

But my Old Firm red card – and again the referee seemed to be swayed by a baying home crowd – was small beer compared to the next match with Celtic, at Ibrox. It was 17 October 1987. This game hit the headlines all around the world. I was not in the team, but I looked on from the Ibrox bench as Frank McAvennie, Celtic's striker and a Scotland teammate of mine, got involved in our area with goalie Chris Woods and Terry Butcher. There were just seventeen minutes on the clock at this stage. I did not think there was much in it either way, but referee Jim Duncan decided to send off McAvennie and Chris Woods, and booked Terry.

We were down to ten men with no substitute goalkeeper, so Graham Roberts took the gloves and did a really decent job. Celtic then went 2–0 up through Andy Walker and an own goal from Butcher, before my captain – who was clearly having a right good afternoon – was booked again and consequently sent off. So, we were now down to nine men, with one centre half in the dressing room and the other in the goal. Interesting, to say the least. But then, incredibly, McCoist scored and Richard Gough grabbed a late equalizer, making the draw feel like a win. The home support were euphoric and all the songs of praise – some appropriate, some not so – were cascading down from the stands. And then Roberts decided to conduct the choir. Hands raised and waving. Everything bar the baton.

Three days later, the Procurator Fiscal in Glasgow decided to order an inquiry and eventually our three players – including our band leader – and McAvennie were charged with a breach of the peace. It was just ridiculous that the game was not allowed to police itself. The Fiscal should have stayed out of a case that was soon tagged – given Frank's bleached blond hair – 'Goldilocks and the Three Bears'. Instead, the man in question, Sandy Jessop, triggered the action against all four players. When it first went to court in December 1987, none of the players were in attendance and the solicitor Len Murray, representing the Rangers contingent, entered a plea of not guilty. I believe that McAvennie also entered the same plea. But the case was deferred, with a new date set for 7 January 1988. Again, Murray entered a not guilty plea, after which a trial was set for February, although it didn't actually take place until 12 April.

The sheriff presiding at the court was Archie McKay and he was advised that the behaviour of the players had triggered scenes between the rival fans at the game – hence the breach of the peace charges. And the Assistant Chief Constable said that incidents on the park had a direct consequence on events in the stands. The players were utterly bemused. In a moment of sanity, the referee Jim Duncan argued that the law should not be getting involved and that if every red card led to a breach of the peace charge, he would retire. He was right and the whole scenario was beyond belief. It was the first prosecution of its type within Britain.

Eventually Chris Woods was found guilty and fined £500 and Terry Butcher found guilty and fined £250. Macca was found not guilty and Roberts received the uniquely Scottish verdict of not proven. 'Not proven' is now a redundant term, having been binned from use by the courts quite recently.

Anyway, only in Scotland could this kind of madness unfold. The way the farce dragged on for months meant that the players, whose names were never out of the newspapers or off the television and radio, had it on their minds all that time. There was a constant reminder from the supporters. It was massive and unnecessary pressure. It was some story, and again the media were doing big business on the front pages and bulletins' lead stories.

It was all insane. I felt so sorry for the players. Butcher and Woods, two of the loveliest guys you could meet, now had criminal records and were spread all over the wrong end of the papers. And Frank McAvennie, one of the good guys whose company I enjoy to this day, should never have got a different verdict from our lads. In truth, none of them should have been in court. It was crazy that the police would act and not allow the Scottish Football Association to handle it.

But let me clear something up here. It has been rumoured for years that the Celtic board would not get a lawyer for Frank and that at my insistence we took him under our umbrella with Len Murray. That is utter and complete nonsense. Why on earth would we have done that?

As for Graham and his Glenn Miller impersonation, I am not so sure he realized about all the songs he was conducting. He might have had an idea about the rivalry between the two clubs and its history, but the English lads really did not get the deep significance of it all. I am from Edinburgh and there were huge swathes of it that I did not really get. I think I had an understanding but no comprehension of the seriousness. And yet it was extremely easy for the players to get wrapped up in it. I always tried to resist that.

When the dust settled, it meant we were four points

behind Celtic with just a point from the first two Old Firm games of the season. I knew the season was going to be difficult. We made some signings around Christmas, but some were stocking fillers. Terry was to be a huge loss after he broke his leg. He was just such an important part of the team by now.

It was the worst season I had at Rangers and it was the price on the ticket . . . that second place is failure. And we could not even manage that. We ended up twelve points behind Celtic and trailing Hearts by two. There was just that League Cup win to show for our efforts.

I had a lot of thinking to do, but at RFC you should always expect the unexpected. You wait for one revolution, and then several come along at once . . .

6

Men of Steel: Murray and Durrant

In the summer of '88, Glasgow hosted a national Garden Festival on the banks of the Clyde, a short stroll from Ibrox. It attracted 4.3 million visitors and put the city back in the international spotlight. Like the nearby club in Govan, the city was undergoing a bit of a rebirth.

Meanwhile, everything in the Rangers garden was far from blooming lovely, and I was sitting my players down and telling them we could not carry on like this. We could not wilt at the first sign of autumn. We needed to be a team of consistent winners. It was not in my plans to alternate the title with Celtic. We could not change with the seasons. There was a drive and determination inside me, a fire that drove me on. I was still in my mid-thirties, with all the energy that brings. We needed to get our championship back and, to do that, things would have to change.

But I had little idea just how much. What happened next was a season of revolutions . . . and then some.

The levels of passionate interest in the well-being of Glasgow Rangers are nothing short of extraordinary – every beat of the Ibrox heart is monitored around the entire world. We have support flung far and wide because of the Scots' tradition of taking their lives elsewhere but never forgetting their roots. But the club – any club – is only as good as its custodians at any given time, and in my reign at Ibrox I was blessed with two fabulous chairmen.

I have already expressed my gratitude and admiration for David Holmes, representing owner Lawrence Marlborough. What happened next redirected the ship. I was introduced to a basketball player by the name of Alton Byrd, who was a British American and – as it happened – not that tall for a basketball player. We both had contracts with Adidas and the company's rep took me to see him play for Livingston, a professional basketball team founded by steel magnate David Murray, who was growing a big reputation as a high-flying businessman. Through that sequence of events, I was introduced by Alton to David. That is where our friendship began.

He had started making his fortune by the age of twenty-three, when he formed Murray International Metals

Limited, dealing in steel distribution, mining and property development. I was immediately impressed with the fortitude, attitude and courage of a man who had been involved in a horrific car accident in 1976 in which he had lost both his legs. His disability did not stop him being super successful. He accepted his lot, rolled up his sleeves and got on with life. His single-mindedness either came from the accident or was something he already had which stoked up his courage to get through the horror of it all. Only on one single occasion did I see him feel a bit sorry for himself, when we happened to be in an airport lounge and perhaps overindulged on the fine wine. But never before or after.

He was right into his sport and that was why he had started and run the basketball team, although rugby was his first love. We became friends and grew the relationship to such a level that we often had dinner together. And when we did sit round a table, David used to laugh at my eating habits. I do like my food and had very much got into the Italian way of dining, with plenty of pasta, garlic and red wine. But I retained a couple of idiosyncrasies. For instance, the restaurant La Parmigiana at Kelvinbridge in Glasgow, which used to stay open late sometimes so I could eat there after midweek games, owned a fish and chip shop next door. I'd sit down at La Parmigiana but would ask them to bring me a single fish from the chippie as a starter . . . which I concede isn't exactly the Italian way! I did not like the fish and chips down south, so I never had them at Liverpool. But it was a different story in Glasgow, where they know how to batter a fish . . . which is why I made this seemingly strange choice.

Anyway, I digress. You could see the passion in David's eyes and his enthusiasm to succeed was clearly evident. He was an ambitious man, and I loved that, so I would bring him along to games. The first game he attended as my guest was the infamous Goldilocks and the Three Bears Old Firm match, so I think he quickly understood what Rangers were all about. Soon after, he told me that he was thinking of buying Ayr United, his hometown team, and while I got that it was something a successful man would want to do, I did ask him: why?

They were his boyhood team, he told me, and he used to travel round the country watching them, but I suggested grander plans. Ayr had had brief moments in the sun in the early seventies under Ally MacLeod, who went on to manage Aberdeen and Scotland, but they were not among the giants of the Scottish game.

Nothing had been said directly between David Holmes and myself, but I was somehow getting the feeling that Lawrence Marlborough was contemplating selling Rangers so he could invest further in what he was doing in America. But at that point, in the spring of 1988, it was just a feeling. In any case, I shared what I felt with David Murray. Although I was just flying a kite, I was also trying to encourage him to think big. Why buy Ayr United when you can have Glasgow Rangers? As it happened, he already advertised his companies trackside at Ibrox in front of what was then the Govan Stand.

Again, I must underline that when it comes to chairmen, David Holmes was as good as it gets, and so I had no qualms about eventually approaching him and explaining what I suspected.

Turns out, I was right. Lawrence wanted out, and Murray's interest was the perfect scenario.

It suited the seller down to the ground because there would be no searching for purchasers, no commissions to be paid, and I could speak for both sides.

The two Davids met and it was smooth as silk. Everyone was happy, none more than me. I was swapping one friend for another, and I knew that the relationships in all directions were rock solid. David Murray took control at Ibrox for £6 million . . . although he also inherited debts of £5 million.

He officially became a director on 22 November 1988, and sat in the main stand as part of the club for the home game against Aberdeen four days later. We won 1–0. I privately advised him not to become chairman immediately, and to keep David Holmes in place for the time being.

I just felt that no matter how successful you have been in the business world, you will find that football is totally different. Many super-rich businesspeople fail to understand how unusual, complex and demanding football is. David Murray was a good listener. He later thanked me and admitted that I was right. It would have been too much of a leap. One step at a time.

Of course, Murray had his basketball team, but this was on a different level. But he was a quick learner because he was intelligent. He absorbed advice like a sponge, and he acknowledged that to wait a bit was the thing to do.

That is what happened, and with my involvement in the deal I became the second-largest shareholder and a director. Life was moving fast yet again. And this was a deal built on one key factor. Trust.

The club changed hands, and within six months Murray stepped up and I had a new chairman, but I will never forget what David Holmes did for Glasgow Rangers and how he understood the club and its support. He had vision at an awkward time in the history of our great institution and saw a way to go out. And he believed in me, a young guy still in his playing days. (When it was said that the 39-year-old Russell Martin was too young to take the job, please recall that I wasn't even that age when I left after five years in the post!) I will be eternally grateful to the man. And so too should the support.

In any case, David Murray set off on the next phase of the journey, and he had a simple mantra: 'Leave the business to me and I'll leave the football to you.' That lasted about a fortnight! But I accepted that he had bought the club and they were his millions. It was just David being David. And we quickly developed an understanding.

It was convenient that we both lived in Edinburgh, and by this time I had moved out of my dad's and into my new home in Colinton. I could see the chairman most days, popping into his office in the Gyle, from where he controlled his empire. It was on the west side of the capital, on my way home from Glasgow. This also meant we would sometimes go together for an early supper. David insisted on a lot of commercial changes at the club, like making the catering in-house for example, and income grew as business boomed with the demand to see the new, successful Rangers. In his time as chairman he organized the construction of a third tier on the main stand, thereby upping the ground's capacity by 7,500. Those sure were interesting times.

Our new owner told me he had taken a call from the infamous newspaper tycoon Robert Maxwell, who owned the Mirror Group at the time. Maxwell had dabbled with Oxford United, whom he had tried to merge with Reading into a team called the Thames Valley Royals, and Derby County. But this time, Maxwell declared he wanted to purchase Rangers from David Murray. That would have been groundbreaking enough, but here was a guy who also wanted to buy Celtic, then merge the two clubs with possibly the biggest rivalry in world football. I have heard some hare-brained ideas in my time but I would like to have seen how that worked out! Can you imagine how both sides of the Old Firm support would have reacted? I had learned that with people like Murray the abnormal becomes normal. Although even he thought Maxwell's idea was insane.

And our chairman did live his life in extraordinary style. David had a house on Jersey in the Channel Islands and we spent a lot of time there, but there was no limit to his jaunts. Every day was an adventure. He owned a stunning home in New Zealand – I can even remember its name, Waimanu – which was a replica of the old South Pacific island houses. It was beautiful. So, one time, he invited me to go there . . . for a Burns supper. The idea was that we'd spend three days in Singapore on the way, so that he could buy furniture for his house in New Zealand. As you do.

We left Ibrox straight after a game and flew to London, where we had to change terminals. As we were sitting in the business lounge, he declared he had changed his mind and wanted to get off the plane and have a night in the capital. But given that our bags were checked through on the flight to the Far East, I persuaded him to carry on with the journey as planned.

It is particularly strange what your memory recalls because I know that Mark Thatcher, son of former prime minister Margaret, was on our flights to and from Singapore, and that he was heading down under to buy a racing car from the great Jack Brabham.

I could not let David snub his fellow Ayrshire man, and so we went to the Burns supper and toasted the Bard, which was just brilliant. As was that whole adventure. To say nothing of others. If you were in the company of that man then you had to be prepared to expect the unexpected.

There was never any bad blood between us. I could say anything to David and vice versa, and nothing was allowed to fester. I was sorry for him for the way it all ended years later, long after I had left the club – Rangers went into financial meltdown and were sold to Craig Whyte for £1 – because I knew David Murray as a man who would move heaven and earth to make Glasgow Rangers successful. In my years working with him, David did nothing but good for the club. He was so emotionally involved in wanting to give the supporters continued success that he stretched the club financially, which was against what his astute business brain usually told him.

But in the 154-year history of Rangers he is the most successful chairman the club ever had. It was a sad ending.

But back to the changes I was making. Graham Roberts had been one of my early signings. Just before Christmas in my first season we gave Spurs more than £500,000 for him and he proved to be worth every penny. Graham became extremely popular with the supporters, and rightly so, because of the way he played. He was totally committed to the club and would take no prisoners. He was made for Rangers. But, to be honest, he became so popular he got carried away with himself. He had of course been involved in the astonishing Old Firm game that ended up in the courts, with teammates Terry Butcher and Chris Woods and Celtic striker Frank McAvennie. It was Graham who had been handed the uniquely Scottish verdict of not proven.

But he sure was guilty of what caused us to fall out and ended his career at Ibrox. Let me say now that if I was given the chance to handle this all over again, I would do it differently. On 30 April 1988 we had played Aberdeen at Ibrox and lost 1–0, and by the time I got back to the dressing room I was spitting feathers. I was having a right go. We had just lost our last home game of the season.

I had said in the match programme that day that I hoped I would never go through another season like the one that was just coming to a close. I blamed Graham for the loss of the goal, and I remember how upset and angry

I was. We had an exchange. And then he told me to fuck off. I could not have that.

So, I told him: 'Tell you what, get a bath, put on your clothes and *you* fuck off. You will never play for Glasgow Rangers again.' And he never did. I sent him with the reserves to all sorts of distant venues around Scotland, where he was an unused substitute. For me, the final nail in the coffin was when, the week after the Aberdeen game, he took his seat among our fans at Falkirk for the last league game of the season. It was his way of showing to the world how popular he was with the support. But it was a challenge to the management team. He was cheered to his seat while I was given abuse on the bench, with even the chairman taking it in the neck too. Graham must have realized this could only go one way. I was never going to tolerate anything like that and the decision to move him on had already been taken. What happened at Brockville that day only made me more resolute.

By the next season he had been sold to Chelsea. And we made our money back. But I got it wrong. I should have told him to come in on the Monday and apologize to his teammates and to me, and then got on with it. I was far too aggressive for my own good. I have told him that since, and in fairness he too accepts he was wrong.

There were others like Robbo. We signed some astonishing characters over the years. Terence Alan Hurlock could fair wind them up. And he became a cult hero with the support. They loved him, but it was a two-way street, as he loved them just as much.

Hurlock was recommended to me by Kenny Dalglish, who had seen him and thought he would do a job for me, so I went to watch him play for Millwall at the Den. I remember it particularly clearly because for some reason television presenter and fellow Scot Kirsty Wark was sitting two seats along from me. I thought she and her husband were Rangers fans, but maybe she had a soft spot for the Lions.

I bought Terry from Millwall for £375,000 in the summer of 1990 and he terrified the opposition, but he was a clean striker of a football and could play. There was one game at Celtic Park where he knocked out two of their players with one challenge so effectively that they stayed down. He then pinged a wonderful forty-yard pass from which we scored. I gave him a thunderous round of applause. It was sensational. I would not have enjoyed playing against him but I liked him a lot. Mind you, I heard he was an interesting bloke to share a night out with. It is probably best as his manager that I never witnessed that.

What I loved about him was that he was fearless and liked to wind up the opposition, something of which I was also sometimes guilty. At Celtic Park at the start of the 1987–88 season, I did my warm-up right in front of the old Jungle at Parkhead, where their most passionate fans were gathered. My back was towards them. I was doing an exercise to stretch my hamstrings that involved bending down to touch my right foot with my left hand and vice versa. What the cameras could not see, but the Celtic fans could, was that I had bared my backside to them. They were going mental. Stark-raving crazy at me. Mind you, they had the last laugh when I was sent off by referee David Syme for a tackle on Billy Stark.

So, we lost our title in 1987–88, with the only thing we had to show for our efforts in that second term being the League Cup triumph. I knew that if you did not learn quickly at Rangers then you would not get to stay on. I also knew, by the start of my third season, that I had a team coming together.

And the message was getting through. By October 1988 we had won our third League Cup in a row after beating Clyde, Clydebank, Dundee, Hearts, and Aberdeen in the final again, this time 3–2. Before that, on 27 August, we had ripped Celtic apart in a 5–1 whipping. The result sent us to the top of the table, where we stayed for the rest of the season. It stunned Celtic. They lost three of their next five league games and went out of the League Cup. We had them in our grip. Before April that season, Rangers had not won in the

East End of Glasgow in nine years, but it took another twelve years before we lost there again.

Given what was on the line, and the fact that the previous season proved we could not take our eye off the ball, I did not want the players to switch off in training, and I would stop games if the intensity wasn't there. We would then do sprints without a ball, which they did not like. They soon realized what to do about it. I needed them to train at match tempo. All our training was aimed at thinking quicker, moving the ball quicker and improving every individual's first touch.

By now I found that I was thinking endlessly about Rangers and its glorious history, the sheer magnitude of the club. My sense of vertigo increased when I realized that, at that point, I was only the eighth man to have been manager in the institution's 116 years, albeit Jock Wallace had held the position twice. Given what has happened since and the turnover rate of managers in the game, that is just a ridiculous statistic. I think I must have learned from the experience. By the end of my career as a manager, I had enjoyed – well, most of them – eight jobs. I was sacked just three times and walked away from the rest. And that, by modern standards, is a fair record.

I had the power to make the lives of Rangers fans better, and I strived to do that in every season. I was learning fast what this club meant to whole families. The passion and devotion were unmatched.

In the 1988–89 UEFA Cup, we played Katowice and won both games. I recall visiting Auschwitz when we played the second leg in Poland and having everything in my life put into perspective. What happened there was truly horrific. In fact, visiting the camp was the most emotional journey I have ever been on. The Nazis tried to exterminate the Jewish people. They also persecuted many others, such as Roma, Slavs, political opponents and people with disabilities. Between 1939 and 1945, the Nazis murdered 6 million Jewish victims. I felt like anyone else who has visited Auschwitz. You want to question mankind. It is incredible to me that anyone should doubt the Holocaust. It is all deeply disturbing.

We lost the second round against Cologne 3–1 on aggregate, with our goal coming from new signing Kevin Drinkell, £500,000 worth of striker from Norwich who finished as our top goalscorer that season. He was a fine old-fashioned centre forward and a good citizen, and you always knew what you would get with him. Not often a nine out of ten, but always a seven or an eight. We sold him to Coventry for a £200,000 profit after a single season

I knew I needed a centre forward and I had tried to persuade Mark Hateley to join us from AC Milan, but somehow he was more tempted by the French Riviera and a contract with Monaco than by the Costa del Clyde, and we had to wait to get him. More on that to come. We had a great season without him, though . . . and, for the lion's share of the season, without Ian Durrant too.

I recall, on the bus heading to Pittodrie that October afternoon in 1988, Ian mentioned that he thought that 'Simmy', the Aberdeen midfielder Neil Simpson, 'might well try to do me today'. He seemed to know something.

Even three seasons in, the animosity the Aberdeen fans showed us could still surprise me. Every time we played at Pittodrie my brother Billy seemed to be given the same seat in the directors' box. Billy is a mild-mannered sort of guy, but this riled him because it meant he was always sat beside the same idiot in the first seat outwith the box, an idiot who spent the entire match shouting abuse at me. They did not like me there. Just as well it was not my other brother, Gordon. He has an even shorter fuse than me. Strange but true.

The atmosphere was horrible that day. Aberdeen won 2–1, with our goal coming from their former player Neale Cooper and one of theirs from our former midfielder Jim Bett. Charlie Nicholas scored their other goal, but in light of events it did not matter really.

Eight minutes into the game, the ball came loose after a series of fierce challenges from both sides. Durrant and Neil Simpson went for it, except Simpson swung his right boot like an axe, smashing it high into Durrant's leg. I have watched Neil Simpson's tackle again and again. It is horrific, and unbelievable that referee Louis Thow allowed the Aberdeen player to stay on the park, a point underlined by Terry Butcher, who put his boot through the referee's door, an action which resulted in a £500 fine. I also seem to recall that Simpson had a go at Durrant earlier in the game. I still think it must have been a deliberate attempt to properly injure our player.

The other thing that still puzzles me is that Ian was light on his feet and normally would have known not to get caught on his standing foot. Over the years, I had tried to be physical with the likes of Zico and Diego Maradona, but they knew to get themselves in the air when something was coming their way. Ian had that built into his game, because he was the sort of player who was destined for the stars. At the time, Rangers were as big as any club in Britain, and he was in love with his boyhood team, but ultimately he could have gone to Real Madrid or Barcelona or Bayern Munich. He was that good. He was destined to be a great player with incredible power and an energy which meant he was still running as fast and hard after ninety minutes as he was in minute one. He would have been especially successful in Italy, where the strikers were so tightly man-marked. He was a midfielder with an ability to arrive late in the box and score goals. David Platt made an enormous success of it over there, but he was the poor man's Ian Durrant.

That evil challenge from Simpson had ripped Ian Durrant's cruciate ligament.

It put him out of the game for nearly three years and further soured relations between Rangers and Aberdeen. After the injury, Durrant became an unbelievably focused individual. So many months of turning up in the gym every day, way before the other players arrived, and staying way after they had left, working on his recuperation. His determination and resilience were astonishing. I never once heard him complain, and anyone who meets him knows he has an incredibly special personality. I do not believe that even once when he put his head on the pillow at night did he feel sorry for himself. He kept up his spirits and those of others, and continued to take the piss out of everyone, including me.

To this day, everyone loves Ian Durrant. He did manage to come back, and enjoyed a great deal of success, but he lost his formative years and never became the player he could have been. He never got the career he deserved. He later sued Simpson and settled out of court. But the whole affair was a terrible injustice.

Durrant was stoic and maybe the team was inspired to win the championship for him because, after wobbling a bit following that match, we then went on a run that saw us drop a single point in twelve fixtures. We were champions for the second time in three years, and were left with the opportunity to earn Rangers a first treble since 1978 by winning the Scottish Cup.

We beat Raith Rovers, Stranraer, Dundee United and St Johnstone – with a replay or two involved – before meeting Celtic in the final. Joe Miller scored the only goal of the game, but it came from a throw-in that should have been ours, which meant we were caught out of position. Referee Bob Valentine also denied us a late equalizer from Terry Butcher, for an apparent foul by Davie Cooper on their goalkeeper, Pat Bonner.

By the time we got to the Hampden dressing room after a game in which I came on as a substitute, I was furious. Over the next eight seasons, this squad would embark on a run unmatched in Rangers' history, a run that would see our club win fifteen of the twenty-four domestic trophies on offer. But at that moment I could only see what was happening right then: we had just lost a cup final to Celtic. I could not contain my anger. I recall hurtling my runners-up medal into the shower area and telling the players, 'I don't collect these,' and that Celtic had better brace themselves for the storm that was coming their way. No one asked for an explanation, and I did not go beyond that. But inside my head it was like an explosion in a fireworks factory.

I could hear the Celtic songs coming from their dressing room and the celebrations around Hampden that afternoon, but I knew something. I knew that I was nursing a secret that would ignite Scottish football and bring a gasp of collective disbelief.

Especially from the Celtic support . . .

7

The Strange Case of the Goalkeeper and the Motorbike

We never stopped the hunt for players who would make us better. We were relentless in our search. We were a management team in a hurry.

I tried and failed to sign my World Cup teammate Jim Bett, who had previously played for the club. I thought he was a very cultured player and a lovely bloke. Hearts centre half Craig Levein was another one who got away, in this case because their chairman, Wallace Mercer, would not do business with us. Scottish clubs, you will recall, had an issue dealing with Rangers.

And here is one for you. I talked to Johan Cruyff about Ruud Gullit, who was with PSV Eindhoven at the time, but the great man told me that we had little chance of getting him because the big Italian clubs were circling . . . and sure enough, he went to AC Milan.

That would have lit the place up! It would have been

some signing, but we never limited our ambitions and would travel anywhere in Europe if we got a tip-off about a potential signing. I was fully committed to my great club, morning, noon and night.

I was always looking for a full back, and several came and went, but Stuart Munro always saw them off the premises. I had inherited him from Jock Wallace, who had bought him from Alloa Athletic, and despite my signings Stu just kept upping his game. He eventually chalked up 179 appearances for Rangers. It makes me smile when I think about him. I always wanted more from Stu when we were attacking and I was never sure about his delivery in the final third, but Walter always championed him because he could see that he was a real defensive asset.

I was too demanding of him and other players. I had expectations that went beyond their capabilities. And I was 100 per cent at fault. It was all to do with the success I had known at Liverpool, which meant that I did not realize how to handle certain players. Sometimes they needed a cuddle, and I was not capable of that as a manager. I always took the other road. Walter argued that the expectation levels of managers who had reached the top of the game as players were too high; they expected every other player to get there too.

Stuart was a fine player and a great guy. And yet I always seemed to be hunting for a left back. Tony Dorigo of Leeds United was another one I fancied. Mind you, I thought I had signed one of the best full backs in the world – if not *the* best.

I had called Nottingham Forest's Brian Clough one evening to ask about the availability of Stuart Pearce, and to my surprise and delight Cloughie agreed to sell him to us. He told me to phone back the following afternoon to discuss it further. I could hardly contain my excitement, but when I did call the great man back, he said he had no recollection of the call and that Psycho – as he was affectionately known – was not for sale at any price. And that I was to fuck off!

There was only one Brian Clough.

Frank McAvennie I liked, but he would not entertain the idea; in any case, I often wonder how, had he signed, I would have policed him and his social life alongside McCoist and Durrant.

Newspaper interest in the nocturnal activities of football players (and managers) had changed after the 1978 World Cup in Argentina, I think, when news reporters started sticking their noses into an area that was once the domain of football writers. All earlier bets were off.

I had issues with them. The photographers could not see over the seven-foot walls I had round my home in Edinburgh, but one afternoon they circumvented that issue with a helicopter that hovered above my house to see who I was entertaining at a barbecue.

Turns out we were not just giving a rebirth to Rangers; we were refuelling the Scottish tabloid newspaper industry. They were such exciting times. Scottish football and its media must have woken up every Monday morning wondering what on earth Souness was going to trigger this week. For the newspapers it was like going back to their golden years – the time decades earlier when they had sold hundreds of thousands of copies daily on the back of the nation's passion for football. For a long time, circulations had been dwindling, but everything we were doing at Ibrox was triggering a revival for the tabloids.

I did not see any of this coming, nor did I want it. For a while I tried the low-profile approach, but it was not me and so I gave up. But there was a price to pay for this freedom. My car was often followed along the M8 motorway, to and from work, and I knew the press would go into restaurants I frequented and ask the staff about who I had been with or what I was doing. I knew because the owners and staff told me. By this time, I had stopped playing and I was not staying in at night watching *Coronation Street*. It was mid-eighties Britain, and I was living the life of a single man after separating from my first wife. I learned to get out of town and go down to London a lot to enjoy my social life.

Meanwhile, as the search to improve Rangers went on, there was another player I tried to buy long before he did come to the club. Andy Goram had a mushrooming reputation at Hibs. Although I had been a teammate of Goram's in the 1986 World Cup squad, I tapped him after bumping into him in an Indian restaurant in Edinburgh in my last season at Rangers. He agreed to come at the end of the season, but two weeks later I got a call from him asking if he could have an advance on his signing-on fee. It was a considerable sum. He was still under contract to Hibs, so of course the arrangement would have to be in hard cash. I decided to take the situation to the chairman, but David Murray said he wanted nothing to do with it. And, furthermore, that he did not even want to know how I intended to proceed. Fair enough.

So I considered the situation and decided to go for it. I arranged to meet Andy one night outside Tynecastle High School, near where I was now living in a flat. I finished an early dinner with David Murray in an Italian restaurant in the West End of Edinburgh that we used to frequent. As we came out, I noticed in my peripheral vision a motorbike, unusually not with a traditional square registration plate, but a long rectangular one like a car. Ah, the experienced midfielder's ability to scan everything around him.

'That's strange,' I remember thinking to myself. David then drove me home to get the money. I picked up the cash, which was in an envelope – a large one – and set off in my own car on the short drive to Tynecastle. But at the end of my street, before I turned on to Corstorphine Road, the main drag, I spotted the bike again. Its rider was talking to someone through an open car window. I reckoned that this guy was clearly waiting for me.

Sure enough, as I turned at the lights just as they were changing to amber, he followed, jumping the red. At this I decided to body-swerve my appointment and take my stalker on a tour of Saughton, where I was brought up.

I knew every road round there like the back of my hand. But he kept on my tail. I even stopped at a petrol station where, despite my tank being nearly full, I squeezed in about £3 worth of fuel. I then phoned my brother Billy and told him to get to my place as quickly as possible. He lived nearby. But by the time I got home, and Billy had met me, the biker had disappeared and I never saw him again. He clearly got the message that I was on to him and that I had called for backup.

After that, I decided not to go through with the deal.

I spoke to Andy about it years later, but he denied all knowledge of anything to do with the evening's events. However, even now, I still think it was all a bit peculiar. And clearly Andy never got the money. It was all very strange, and the goalie is no longer with us to give his side of it. In any case, he went on to become a Rangers legend.

Of course, we still had not signed a high-profile Catholic, but please do not think it was all I lived for and planned. Or that I was on a mission. That is just not the way it was. We wanted talented players, that was that. I did not give a toss about their religion.

If we go back to my first press conference, it had never crossed my mind that I would be asked about the faith of the players I might or might not sign, because I just never saw it as an issue. Call me naive, but that kind of stuff wasn't part of my world. When I said that signing Catholics wasn't a thorny question to me, I wasn't being brave, just honest about how I felt about the insanity of it all. Religion – in football – is such an unimportant thing.

My then-wife was a Catholic and so were my kids. It just did not exist as an issue for me and, truth be told, I did not really understand the fuss. It had not been on my radar when I was at school in Edinburgh. Why would it be? Sectarianism was much more part of the west of Scotland's culture.

This meant that although Peter Marinello – who went on to play for Hibs and Arsenal – went to a different school to me because his family were Catholic and mine were Protestant (him to St Joseph's and me to Broomhouse), we shared the same pitch as part of a local team. And a football friendship.

Years later, not one person at Ibrox ever challenged me about the position I'd taken regarding signing a Catholic, although I am sure there were one or two about the place who thought it was not a particularly clever idea. And I *knew* there were two or three in the dressing room who were not comfortable with my plans. But imagine where Rangers would be now had we not done something. And do we really think that UEFA and FIFA would not have turned their attention to the situation in the modern world?

But, to be honest, I was too busy to have time to think about the pressure to stick to traditions. I was just working hard trying to make Rangers better. My own playing time was thinning out and a moment at training when Ian Ferguson – who was a fabulous player for Rangers – totally out-muscled me when I thought I was in control of the ball was a wake-up call that life was moving on. It was an early warning bell that maybe I was, after all, getting on a bit. Perhaps that's why I was directing more of my time and energy towards being a manager than I was to being a player.

During the 1988–89 season I made just ten appearances as a player, only six of which were in the league. I knew the end was nigh in the dressing room. I recall the cup final in which we were trying to complete a domestic treble. I agonized over my team selection, which I did not announce until we were getting stripped.

Andy Gray had been signed on a free transfer from West Brom that season and was only ever going to be a bit-part player for us, because he was near the end of a fabulous career. But he was a Rangers man through and through – a Glasgow lad – and he thought all his Christmases had come at once when I offered him a deal. Andy was from Drumchapel, a housing scheme in the city, but had made his name at Dundee United before moving to Aston Villa and other big clubs in England. He had been a top striker.

In those days there were only two substitutes, and, having picked a starting line-up that included Ally McCoist and Kevin Drinkell up front and a strong selection all over, I agonized over whether to put Andy on the bench alongside Davie Cooper . . . or my good self. He was already taking off his tie and undoing his shirt, and he clearly expected a place in the technical area, but I picked myself to sit next to Coop. Andy, I think, was devastated, and I can see his disappointed look even now, but I was paid to make decisions and that was the one I took.

There was no hiding place from the world back then. The institution that was Glasgow Rangers had me fired up to feed the support the success they craved and genuinely believed was their right. I could sleep at night but I was totally focused on making the club better and better.

It can be a hard shift and, wonderful though it is, there is a limited time in the job at Rangers . . . and Celtic. It is born of our dominance, and the shared dislike from the rest of the football community in Scotland, jealous of what we have achieved.

Years later, I can recall offering advice to Martin O'Neill when he became manager of Celtic for the first time. I told him he should wear a suit in the technical area and not a tracksuit, because he, like me, was showing too much emotion on the touchline. I felt that wearing a suit had a calming effect.

As I said, I tried to be humble at first, but it became obvious to me that this was not the way to go. These two jobs are the most stressful in British football. The pressure is intense and the demands on your life and that of your family make it hard to live a normal existence. But I know that I am one lucky man. You are blessed to have one career, but I have had three . . . and the phone still rings.

The passion for our club is incredible, and something that is passed down from generation to generation. I find it interesting that people who support the club are nearly always described as 'big' Rangers fans. It's as if the adjective is compulsory. But it underlines exactly how they feel. It is consuming. It is their way of life.

Meanwhile, something else was about to consume

my life. Looking back, without realizing it at the time, the issues I had inherited that would later lead to me having open-heart surgery had begun to impact on me. On match days, when the players went out for their warm-up, Donald Cruickshank, our club doctor, would take my blood pressure, which was always extremely high. I put it down to the excitement of the matches. But, in truth, I was living with a ticking bomb. There was something dangerous inside my body.

For about three years, I'd been getting raging headaches, and I was virtually living on Solpadeine, a painkiller drug available over the counter. I was never a big drinker, but I would take the pills before I went out, when I came back home, and again in the middle of the night. And before I set off for training at Ibrox.

What was happening was a narrowing of my arteries thanks to a build-up of plaque. At no stage did I have a heart attack, but hypertension and something called low-density lipoprotein were creating something that would turn out to be a problem for me. It was in my genes, and even my fitness levels could not beat it.

My dad had open-heart surgery at the age of seventy-two and had lost two of his brothers in their mid-thirties to the same issues, so there was every chance that I had inherited the dodgy genes. The condition, the problem, are not rare in Celtic people (that's the nations, not the team). I will be eternally grateful to all the medical talents who worked on me, and for the existence of the British Heart Foundation, for whom I became an ambassador a long time ago. That and my work as vice president of DEBRA – a national organization supporting people with epidermolysis bullosa, a just evil condition – consume my work for charities.

At Rangers, all this was percolating in my body and maybe I was too aggressive and too confrontational at times, which exacerbated my condition. But I want zero sympathy from anyone.

Things were getting to me. I had a feeling that we were getting shafted. I realized that some people were out to snare me, whether it was the press or the authorities.

There was an incident in February 1990 when the television people at STV stitched me up, pointing their cameras to catch the top of my head in the tunnel at a game against Hearts while I was serving a touchline ban. I was trying to pass on tactical instructions.

The SFA then extended the suspension using STV's pictures as evidence. As a result, we fell out with the television company and banned them from Ibrox. It was my decision but no one at the club objected to it. What STV interpreted as 'good journalism' – in other words, 'let us get Souness into trouble' – was just a case of them highlighting everything to the Scottish Football Association.

But then they would come to us asking for interviews and co-operation. They still expected access all areas – in their eyes, nothing had changed. Well, not in mine.

It was madness the way I was treated, and, at times, it was just ridiculous. My celebratory sprint on to the pitch when we later won the League Cup at Hampden for the final time with me as manager was seen as a violation of the touchline ban.

I also felt the small-minded officials who had infested the Scottish Football Association at the time were trying to put every barrier in our way, and that there was a small-town mentality in Scottish football generally. I had lived most of my life away from the country and realized how parochial some people in officialdom could be. The national association banned me from the touchline for an unprecedented *two years*. How can you have a two-year ban? It was scandalous. And it suggested to me that we were being treated differently.

Being at Rangers gave me a feeling of huge respect and affection from the support, which extends to this day. It's way beyond anything at even Liverpool, but outside our fantastic backing, life was becoming more difficult. I was appearing more on the front pages of newspapers than the back. My private life was fodder for the tabloids more than the football was at times, and I did not like it. The level of intrusion into my privacy was completely out of proportion and seemed to obscure coverage of what was most important: what was happening on the park.

You cannot be invisible, but I had been taught at Liverpool to never get too big for my boots and to respect the city. There was a lot going on there in the early eighties. In Glasgow the scrutiny was even more intense, and Rangers players were put on a pedestal. Luckily, not many got carried away. Maybe one or two, but they were the exceptions. All of this was going on around me and – although unknown at the time – inside me.

I should have heeded David Murray's advice; he was always telling me to take a couple of days off and get out of Scotland. He told me that if I did that I would see the job and problems very differently. He was sure I would get a clearer picture. I seldom did, although some of my socializing was done seeing old friends in Middlesbrough or Merseyside or London, so that gave me some respite, even if it wasn't focused on rest.

But on one occasion I did take his advice and headed off for a few days to Champneys health farm in Hertfordshire. I was offered all sorts of treatments, but when the doctor checked me over on my first examination, and realized how high my blood pressure was, he excluded me from the vast majority of them. It was so high they would not allow me to use the sauna or go to the steam room. My blood pressure was through the roof. It was a total waste of money because there was nothing in which I could indulge. I just slept for three days. I could have stayed in the house!

Maybe at that point something should have clicked.

Looking back, I did not have an off switch. That's probably still true now, to be honest. My mum used to point to me and say to my brothers and anyone who cared to listen, without using my name, that I could not sit down and 'There is something wrong with that one. He's got ants in his pants.'

I am happy to admit that a lot of the pressure back then was self-inflicted. It was the fear of failure, the fear of a loss of credibility. And any failure would be reflected on your family. I always remember the look on my dad's face when I was sent off on day one at Easter Road. You want everyone around you to be proud of what you do. I think that applies to all of us.

I always wanted to be as successful a manager as I was as a player, and a tally of eleven trophies in three countries is a fair return. From my vantage point now I can see that it probably wasn't realistic to think that as a coach I could match the days of silverware I enjoyed as a Liverpool player. But it was still an incredible period of my life.

I recall one evening in 1989 in David Murray's office, working late into the night with an English businessman called Michael Knighton and a group of lawyers who were negotiating to buy the majority shareholding in Manchester United. Knighton had somehow convinced the United chairman, Martin Edwards, to give him an option to buy his shares. The deal was agreed in the early hours, and David and I went back to his house, where he woke up his wife Louise to make us bacon and eggs. Those who were around at the time will confirm that Rangers were every bit as big a club as the Old Trafford outfit. We were certainly outbidding them for players in the transfer market. Alex Ferguson was yet to unveil his golden generation of Beckham, the Nevilles, Butt, Scholes and Giggs.

The problem was that Knighton did not have sufficient funds in his company to back up the bid, and so he had offered the Rangers chairman a slice of the action. David always kept me up to speed with his Rangers business, and again he included me in the conversation. David had decided to go for it and suggested to me that I might want to become the United manager. Quite the idea. But I was the former captain of Liverpool – I don't know how that would have gone down. Well, maybe I do . . . The plan was that I would move to Manchester and Walter would take over at Ibrox.

David had a vision of a commercial merger in which Rangers and United could jointly benefit in terms of jersey sponsors, trackside advertising and the like. It was all remarkably interesting and revolutionary. It was a groundbreaking idea to harness together two massive football clubs. Quickly it became clear that Knighton did not have the money to do the deal, but that David did and could.

In any case, the following morning our chairman changed his mind because of two factors. The SFA and the Scottish League informed him that without doubt it was impossible to become a major shareholder in two British clubs. It was totally against the rules. He also decided all his love, time and commitment should be dedicated to Rangers. In retrospect, it was his biggest business mistake, given Manchester United's current value of circa £5 billion.

As the decade drew to a close, my life was on fire. I just never knew what was going to happen next. But you know what? If you were to offer me the chance to experience everything that has happened to me up till now all over again, I'd sign up tomorrow. And anyway, the fun had only just begun . . .

8
Mo

There is a majesty and a sense of history about the main entrance at Ibrox. There's the portrait of Alan Morton – the Wee Blue Devil – that hangs over the glorious marble staircase, which in turn winds its way up to the manager's office and the renowned Blue Room that has hosted so many gatherings of the game's famous.

Rangers fans know its traditions. It's where new managers are unveiled, where hospitality is handed out and where meetings are held under murals of the club's history painted by the incredibly talented artist Senga Murray – her work is a reflection of the respect that Rangers command. It is also the place the annual Loving Cup ceremony is held, a tradition dating back nearly a century where the health of the monarch is toasted.

Its atmosphere grabs me every time. I just pause and look. It is a room with majesty.

The club is about tradition, much of it coming from

the great Bill Struth, who was manager from 1920 until 1954. He insisted on standards way above those other clubs looked for. He cultivated a winning mentality and encouraged fair play. Players had to wear collar and tie – even to training – and they also had to put on bowler hats. He created the Rangers image.

He was famous for his speeches: 'To be a Ranger is to sense the sacred trust of upholding all that such a name means in this shrine of football.' And the legendary: 'We welcome the chase. It is healthy for us. We will never hide from it.' He won eighteen championships, ten Scottish Cups and two League Cups.

In the trophy room and the boardroom you can feel the presence of football giants like Mr Struth who wore the blue and white. I repeat, football giants. Glasgow Rangers is no place for wee boys. History lives here. You can feel it all around you; sometimes it hangs so thick in the air it's like you could cut yourself a slice. And once it gets you, it will never let you go. It is an everlasting love. I never get fed up with that building. It just feels like a proper football club. You can smell the tradition.

But, of course, not all the history was right. All its days, Rangers had refused to knowingly sign Roman Catholics, even if one or two did find their way into the club over the years. The South African Don Kitchenbrand, who played in the fifties, allegedly kept his faith quiet while he was a big favourite of the fans, and in the seventies, Graham Fyfe was given a hard time because he married a Catholic woman. It was unbelievable. John Spencer was another lad who attracted headlines – he was a Catholic who had joined the club as a schoolboy – before he went on to become a star at Chelsea, Queens Park Rangers and Everton, among others.

It was not that I wanted to sign a player of that faith just to scream from the hilltops that things had changed. It was more like I wanted to say: 'Here is a right talented player and he is a Catholic? Oh, is he? So what?'

Mo Johnston I knew as a Scotland teammate. He was an outstanding striker who originally made his name at Partick Thistle, where he scored a goal about every second game, before heading south to Watford. Elton John was the chairman there and Maurice kept up his fabulous strike percentage with twenty-three in thirty-eight games, goals that helped them reach the 1984 FA Cup final. He then moved to his boyhood heroes, Celtic, where he improved on his one-goal-every-two-games average. Mo was a player, all right. He then spent a couple of years with Nantes in France, where he thoroughly enjoyed the lifestyle and became an even better player, before the events of the summer of '89.

It was announced in the press – in early May – that he was going back to Parkhead, and he was pictured at the stadium in a Celtic top with manager Billy McNeill. But then, under curious circumstances, I found out that Celtic had jumped the gun . . . big time. And the fuse was lit on a sensational transfer that would explode everything people thought they knew about Scottish football. It was after a game – that day against Aberdeen when I lost my rag at Graham Roberts – and I was coming down the aforementioned staircase at Ibrox.

Mo's agent, Bill McMurdo, was leaning against one of the radiators at the bottom. I have no recollection as to why he was there, but the news about the player he represented apparently going back to Parkhead had broken. As I walked past him, I just casually said, 'Pity you hadn't told me that, Bill, we would have been interested in him.' Bill pushed himself off the radiator and said, 'Would you really? Well, let me tell you something, he hasn't actually signed yet . . .' I spun round and told him to follow me into my office on the ground floor near the dressing room. It was there that we began a conversation that was to set football ablaze.

Bill explained that his player had a three-year contract at Nantes and, given that this was pre-Bosman ruling, under normal circumstances he would not have been able to let his contract run down and leave for free at its end. But McMurdo had agreed a special arrangement that Mo *could* leave for nothing if he saw out the deal, and so, with a year still to run, Nantes would be keen to recoup a fee now. According to Bill, there was interest from Torino, Stuttgart, Spurs and Montpellier.

What happened next is probably the most written-about, debated, headlined transfer in the history of the game. The tabloids couldn't find a typeface big enough to scream the headlines. I spoke to David Murray, and he agreed we should go for it. We had to agree a deal with Nantes, because we were hijacking Celtic's bid for the player. However, they were keen since Celtic were procrastinating.

The clause that McMurdo had negotiated in Mo's contract would also allow him to be released if a buying club paid the fee. Celtic, it seemed, were messing Nantes about in producing the money. They had let down their defences and we pounced on the opening. We paid the French club Mo's £1.3 million buyout clause and in return we got a bargain.

In my office that afternoon, Bill and I set the entire process in motion, and then, after David Murray gave me his full backing, the snatch of the century was under way. It was like a James Bond film after that. Days later, Maurice and Bill agreed to meet me and Rangers chief executive Alan Montgomery in a café in a suburb of Paris. It was all cloak-and-dagger stuff.

When I set off for the clandestine get-together, I avoided Glasgow, because I knew there were people there reporting my every move to the papers, and flew instead from Edinburgh to London. I then took another flight to Paris, where we met Maurice and Bill in this deserted old Parisian café called Ouazene near Orly Airport, which looked like the set of an episode of *'Allo 'Allo!* Apart from the bar staff, there was not a soul in sight. It was, as they used to say in films, all very hush-hush, and slightly surreal.

Mo and I had spoken several times on the phone by now – he was, remember, a player who had been my teammate on Scotland trips and who needed no introduction to me. He had not seemed to hesitate about coming to Rangers, only wanting to know that we were serious about buying better players and taking the club in the right direction. I reassured him that we were aiming not only to be the best club in Scotland, but in Britain.

Mo later talked about hoping we could conquer Europe. He wanted to be a winner. He was very enthusiastic. His personality was so important in all of this – his ability to be such a cheeky chappy. Mo is a very likeable guy. But I went to Paris because I needed to convince myself that he meant it. I needed to see the colour of his eyes, confirm to myself that this was no false dawn. I had been down this road before with Ray Houghton and John Collins, who both initially said yes but then changed their minds. Mo convinced me immediately, and within an hour I was heading back to the airport, reversing my steps via London to Edinburgh.

Now I was sitting on an atomic bomb of a story that had to be kept from detonating.

The Scottish season was still in full swing, and we still had that cup final against Celtic, the game that we lost and I threw my runners-up medal into the shower area at Hampden in anger. For the record, I played in thirteen cup finals and that was the only one I ever lost. But by then I knew Mo was coming to us, so it did help with the disappointment, even if I had to keep it all secret.

That cup final was on 20 May and we managed to keep the story under lock and key until a press conference fifty days later. It was absolutely astonishing. It was the best-kept and biggest secret ever. Even now I cannot believe it never got out. Not a whisper of anything.

Mind you, there was one narrow escape. Me, Mo, Bill McMurdo and David Murray had a meeting at the chairman's house in Edinburgh, where the garden backs on to a golf course. It was a lovely day, and we were sitting outside chatting, when suddenly a stray ball flew over the wall and minutes later this chap came looking for it. He could not believe his eyes and said so. Bill replied, 'So you didn't see us then,' and told him to get back to the golf. I often imagine what he told the blokes in the clubhouse and wonder if they believed it!

At Rangers, only me, Walter, David, Phil Boersma and club secretary Campbell Ogilvie were in on the story. Bill McMurdo dealt with Nantes and, save for paying the fee, Rangers were not really in contact with the French club. The buyout clause meant that there were no negotiations. Bill had played a blinder.

All these years later, I still wonder at how amazing it was that everyone who was sworn to secrecy was 100 per cent solid. The rumour-mongers just did not get a sniff. And that is hardly how the west of Scotland normally works. When I was at Liverpool, they could keep a signing quiet until the day of the reveal, but that was impossible in Glasgow . . . or at least I thought it was. Not one journalist cracked it all those weeks and it became our story to tell. All of us stayed totally shtum, including the chairman. And congratulations to him, because David always wanted to oversee major announcements. Mo and Bill were surely badgered daily by Billy McNeill about the much-heralded – if prematurely announced – move to Celtic, but still they did not crack. I have no idea how the pair of them kept Celtic at bay all that time. They did not breathe a word and the Celtic management could hardly ask us! Seven weeks of poker faces. Until the big day . . . The whole thing was just incredible.

I knew that even at £1.3 million we had got ourselves a steal. Mo was the right age, had a perfect temperament and was the kind of player who, no matter how much you physically abused him, would always come back for more. He was a big-game player.

I had a recurring, nagging fear that he would change his mind. We stayed in touch and I was praying that I never got a call saying he was rethinking . . . and I never did. He never wavered.

It makes me smile now. Rangers have recently made headlines for appointing two managers – Russell Martin and Danny Röhl – in their thirties. By the time of this explosive signing of Mo, I was the same age Röhl was when I wrote this book . . . except with five domestic trophies under my belt, and more to come. Plus the experience of this history-making bit of business. It puts into perspective what I was going through.

The first inkling the press, the Celtic board and the Celtic fans would have got about the incredible decision Mo had made would have arrived on the day of the announcement – Monday, 10 July 1989. And it must have been like a hornet's nest being kicked. It was mayhem. Mo was smuggled into Ibrox by car, through the gates at the Broomloan Road end of the stadium. For that I'll always be grateful to the late Alistair Hood, our then-head of security, who had the job of covering the player in blankets and sneaking him into the ground in his car. A couple of days ahead of the announcement, I had to inform Alistair that on the Monday we would be unveiling a huge signing and that the security arrangements would have to be beyond anything we had put in place before. But I could not tell him who it was. He took it all in his stride, although I am sure his jaw dropped when Mo emerged from the car and into the main stand, where eventually he was taken into the press conference in the Blue Room, where flashbulbs popped and reporters took a collective deep breath.

In these moments, as the news broke around the country, I am positive that the nation was talking about little else. Actually, I knew from the reaction and press interest that the story was being read around the planet. Expat Scots in Canada, the US, South Africa, Australia and New Zealand were hungry for the news. There were probably people reading about it from Kansas to the Kremlin. At least, that is how it seemed.

Having acted and looked calm and collected at the press conference, Mo was at last taken through a back door and out of Ibrox. Alistair wanted me to go that way too, but I insisted to him that I would leave by the main entrance . . . and I did. I had decided that there would be no sneaking away for me. No change from my normal plans.

There was a large group of fans waiting and a few did set fire to or rip up their season tickets, but I did not find the atmosphere intimidating. I knew what we had done was right and I knew we had got ourselves a brilliant centre forward.

This was preseason and the team were already in Italy, so what happened next was that Maurice and I reconvened at Glasgow Airport and then took a private flight to a tiny airport in northern Italy. We cleared customs there and reboarded the plane en route to Lucca. From there it was on to Il Ciocco, where our squad were gathered for pre-season training. It was here that Mo would be welcomed by his new teammates. Mo of course knew most of them, either from international duty or from playing against them. Or from nightclubs in Glasgow. But when we arrived in time for a meal, they had set out a table for one in the corner of the dining area. McCoist and Durrant would be my chief suspects . . . but as a joke it broke the ice, and it was well received by the new recruit. He fitted in exactly as I expected. And was everything I hoped he would be. Or should I say knew he would be. And the players realized we had upped the ante and underlined our ambition.

Mo, who really was a fabulous player, was a brave boy in what he did. He moved into my house with the high walls in Edinburgh (this was while I still lived there). That had been part of our sales pitch. We promised we would take care of him. The place had two electric gates, and he travelled to Ibrox every day from this home in the capital. His commitment was never in doubt despite the incredible attention. He was a remarkable young man. The club also paid for 24/7 security for him, and I got a good friend of mine, Graham Pederson – a martial arts expert – to look after him when he was out. And he did go out. That blond hair and his gear meant Mo could never be invisible . . . although he thought he was. He had an incredible personality which allowed him to carry on unfazed by the fuss all around him.

Maurice Johnston had everything about him to do this. The personality, the resolve, the ability to be fearless and, most of all, the ability to improve our team. I certainly never harboured a second of doubt or questioned what I was doing. There was only one occasion in all the time he played for me that he ever caused me any concern. That was on his second preseason trip to Il Ciocco in Tuscany, when I let the players have a free night to relax. I had taken my kids with me and had an early bed, and I do recall hearing a bit of commotion, but I decided not to get up and confront any players. I reckoned that they'd had a drink, and confronting young men who have had alcohol could turn messy because I would have wanted the last word.

The next morning, I found out more about the commotion that had disturbed my evening. Too much drink had, of course, been consumed, and a practical joke had gone wrong. Someone – no prizes for guessing who had gone to Maurice's room and removed his mattress to reveal the old-fashioned metal springs that beds used to have. Mo returned to his room worse for wear, did not put the light on, and dived on to what he thought was his mattress, hitting the springs in the process. The first I knew of it was when I was sitting there having breakfast. Mo appears and his face looks like a Bengal tiger has attacked him. And I am thinking, 'How do I explain this one?'

Oh, the joys of managing young testosterone-filled footballers.

I was 100 per cent confident Mo would win over our fans, and he started the process by being about the place for friendlies against Airdrie, Kilmarnock and Partick Thistle, before his Ibrox debut in a friendly against Spurs, a game which we won 1–0.

The goalscorer was Trevor Steven, who was another gloriously successful signing that summer. There were hiccups at the start, but I knew it would come good. At no time did I doubt that we had done the right thing, and I made it clear that it was my decision to go this road – with support from others. But it was my idea.

And I believe the Maurice signing had an unforeseen bonus for us, causing a period of anger between Celtic's board and the club's supporters, who felt let down by what we had done and their own board's dithering. Their fans felt embarrassed by it all. Although by now a huge swathe of them had tagged their former hero as 'Judas', deep in their hearts they knew we had signed a right valuable player and stolen one on their club. That Scottish Cup success in May 1989 would be their last domestic silverware for six years, while Rangers were about to embark on an unprecedented spell of domestic dominance.

Still, it was clear that what I was doing did not have the universal appreciation of everyone. There were a couple of incidents. There were stables at my house and when Maurice was living there someone set them on fire. Also, a group of guys from Special Branch asked to see me at Ibrox and gave me a security briefing. They asked about my lifestyle – what pubs and restaurants I used – and discussed the route I took to the stadium every day from my home in Colinton. They told me to park under streetlights and keep my car in the garage at home at night, and that they would be following me for several weeks. The Edinburgh city bypass was not complete at the time, and I used to go through Wester Hailes, a housing estate close to Broomhouse, where I'd gone to school. Clearly, I knew the area well.

'I'll be fine there,' I told them, but they then informed me that some people they worked with were not happy with this. Apparently, I was going under too many bridges, where there was the possibility of people throwing bricks through the windscreen of my car. I later heard people were arrested in Wester Hailes who were part of a Protestant terrorist organization.

It seems that I had managed to upset *both* sides of the great divide. I did not receive any actual death threats, but I do recall that at several home games there were faces around me in the directors' box that I didn't recognize. Campbell Ogilvie informed me later that they were Special Branch chaps who were nursing increased concerns about my safety.

Mo had his own issues, of course, and sure played his part in upping the circulation of the newspapers. While there were a few that were outraged, the majority were delighted with what we had done. It went both ways, really, and to this day I am still approached by blokes in their late thirties called Graeme – plenty of them – proclaiming they were named after me by proud Rangers-loving parents.

But I can still recall going, early on in my career at Ibrox, to an Old Firm Glasgow Cup game at Hampden. I was outside the ground, wearing a three-quarter length leather coat and a black polo neck, when this guy dragged his boy to within two yards of me and said to his five-year-old: 'Look son, there's the bad man.'

I am not and never have been a big boozer in any case, but I did not want to confront trouble, so I avoided places where alcohol was being served and just visited decent restaurants. Still, there were some strange people about. A few days before Christmas 1990, I had taken delivery of a brand-new Mercedes and I decided to drive through to the stadium on Christmas Day itself for a session in the gym and a sauna before heading on to Leeds. I was going to watch Tony Dorigo play on Boxing Day for United against Chelsea. As it happens, I never did get him for Rangers, although later I took him to Torino. I was still clearly doubting poor Stu Munro!

By this time, I was separated from my first wife and David Murray had invited me for Christmas dinner, but I declined in favour of a drive to Yorkshire and what turned out to be hamburger and chips for one, courtesy of room service cooked by the receptionist at the Holiday Inn! Anyway, as I came off the motorway near Ibrox, there was a guy in the back of a taxi with his arm round his girlfriend. Suddenly he spotted me. The cab stopped at the lights, and he decided to give me every rude hand gesture you could ever think of, and some you could never imagine. I turned into the filling station and by now he has the taxi stopped outside and he has his arse out the window at me. I am thinking to myself, 'What a prick,' and snatch the pump to fill my nice new motor. But I was so distracted by this idiot I had topped up with diesel instead of petrol!

I had to call Mercedes' emergency helpline and explain that I was trying to get to Leeds. They told me to top my car up at every fuel station I came to, and I did get away with it, but that clown was exactly what he was showing out the window. There are few hiding places in the west of Scotland, and clearly a petrol station is not one of them.

I had signed Maurice to play with Ally McCoist and I was aware they knew one another well, on and off the pitch. They had a good understanding. What I understood was that, after a drink, both believed that nobody would recognize them. Although they were not the only two in that dressing room. It is a peculiarly British thing, you know: 'I've had my fifth pint, so you cannot see me now.' Maybe, in that time of madness, I should have tried it. I could have done with disappearing a bit . . .

9
My Way

There is something incredibly special about Ibrox Stadium. The place has an aura.

It was first opened in 1899 – it was known then as Ibrox Park – but it was the legendary work of architect Archibald Leitch that transformed the place with its famous main stand into something unique. The criss-cross balcony and red-brick front of the now listed building pull at the heartstrings of Rangers fans, whether they're exiled or are those who visit on a regular basis. I still feel the sense of belonging and pride in the club when I go through those front doors.

Tradition is so important. For example, it never entered my mind at any point to change the dress rule for players that stipulated they should turn up in collar and tie on training days and match days. Who was I to interfere with 100 years of history, or argue with the founding fathers, who decided this was what would define Glasgow Rangers and set them apart from the others! Rangers were the custodians of Scottish football and its past.

There is no other club that compares to its sense of history and tradition. Ibrox has been worked on and updated over the years, but that main stand and its hallway ooze history in the way no other stadium does. And it was our job to pay homage to those who had given birth to the club. They had wanted certain standards, so it was our job to make sure that they continued to be upheld. Collars and ties and blazers were part of that.

During our time, the great players of another era – Willie Waddell and Willie Thornton – were still around the place, and they were constant reminders of the astonishing past of this great club. And, of course, there had been so few managers of Rangers over the years. William Wilton, Bill Struth, Scot Symon, Davie White, Willie Waddell, Jock Wallace, John Greig, Wallace again and then me. Since 1872, which was 116 years. Just remarkable.

Sadly, it took the 1971 disaster for the then-board to develop a safe, modern stadium, and manager Willie Waddell led the plans to redesign the ground in the style of the Westfalenstadion in Dortmund, Germany. The redevelopment was finished by 1981, and cost the club a fortune – multimillions – which meant that money was not directed at the transfer market. There were priorities, and Rangers led the way among Scottish clubs in stadium rebuild. We were miles ahead of the rest.

Because it became such a beautiful structure, it has played host to all sorts of non-football events over the years, including world championship boxing from the likes of Scotland's Jim Watt, rugby sevens for the Commonwealth Games, and even the centenary of the Boys' Brigade. And concerts by stars like Simple Minds, Rod Stewart, Billy Joel, Bon Jovi and Elton John.

Oh, and Frank Sinatra.

You will forgive me if I take a bow for that one. Ol' Blue Eyes – although I believe he might have been called that before he came to Govan – became Ol' Bluenose on 10 July 1990, on a tour that was a celebration of his seventy-fifth birthday. Superstars do not come much bigger.

Glasgow – which was enjoying being European City of Culture that year – was to be a venue for one of his concerts, and Celtic Park had been selected as the venue. However, I managed to head them off at the pass . . .

At the start of the 1989–90 season we learned that the great man was to come to Glasgow the following summer and perform at Celtic Park. I had a pal called Tony Bruce in London who had the ear of promoter Harold Davidson, and so I suggested they switch to Ibrox because it was state of the art, all-seated and much more comfortable for the clientele who would want to see Sinatra.

Tony agreed to speak to Davidson and they saw my logic and allowed us to hijack the whole concert. First Frank Sinatra taken away from Celtic and later Mo Johnston. It was not a bad double . . .

And so, on a summer night in 1990, after the end of the season, one of the greatest entertainers the world has known rocked up at the stadium. He sang seventeen songs over eighty-three minutes and wowed the crowd. He was nothing short of fabulous. At his afternoon soundcheck he sang only four words, 'come fly with me', and that was him ready.

They set up his stage in front of the Govan Stand and he got changed in the away dressing room of the main stand, before driving across the pitch on a golf buggy. I cannot quite recall why he did not use the home dressing room, where by now I had installed a massive portrait of Her Majesty the Queen.

Back in 1947, when she was still Princess Elizabeth, she visited Ibrox after becoming engaged to Prince Philip, and before that her parents, King George VI and the Queen Mother, had watched a civil defence display there during the war. A couple of years before Sinatra's visit, I had decided that we needed a picture of our queen in the home dressing room and I sent our assistant kitman, George 'Doddie' Soutar, out to find a suitable picture. He came back with one that was bigger than he was, and it stayed up there through my time in office and beyond.

Anyway, for some strange reason, Sinatra was in the other changing room. But I got to meet him and present him with a whisky decanter on behalf of the club. He was absolutely charming, with no airs and graces, although I was aware that I was in the presence of greatness. Honestly, he came across as a sincere superstar. What a talent. It was a stadium he played that night, but he turned it into a nightclub atmosphere. He was a genius.

He loved the decanter and later wrote me this letter.

Dear Graeme,

Thank you for the marvellous gift. It has a special place in our California home.

And the wonderful people of Glasgow will always have a special place in my heart. I was shown so much love and warmth at the Ibrox Stadium concert that I am still overwhelmed by the reception I received.

It is a memory I will always cherish.

Warmest regards, Frank Sinatra.

I read somewhere that he later told his entourage: 'In all my time in showbusiness I have never had such a stupendous feeling. I have never been so moved by anything in my life before.'

But it was not just Sinatra; they have all played Ibrox, and not only musicians.

On holiday one summer in the south of France, I left my room and walked along the corridor towards the lift, where a tall guy was standing but hadn't pressed the call button, and I said to him: 'We won't be going anywhere if you don't push the button, my friend.'

'Oh, sorry,' he smiled, and he asked if I was Scottish. I explained that I was, and he asked me if I had ever heard of Ibrox Stadium and Glasgow Rangers. I indicated that I might have – he had no clue about my identity.

'Great,' he said, 'it is a fabulous place. I performed there once . . .'

Not in a football strip, nor in a rock band, I thought to myself. And I was right.

It was American evangelist Billy Graham, who had preached to tens of thousands in 1955 as part of a six-week stay in Scotland.

If he remembered Ibrox with warmth, think of what it means to the people who were there every day and continue to be so – the Rangers family.

I sit sometimes all these decades on and reflect on how lucky I was to inherit some incredibly special human beings who dedicated their working lives to Glasgow Rangers. People like the wonderful Laura Tarbet, who served as secretary to Rangers managers way before and after me – all the way back to Willie Waddell, I think – a diamond of a woman who understood how the club worked and knew what to tell me and what not to tell me. She protected me from a lot of letters that I really did not need to see. She was Rangers to the core.

Then there were Laura and the women who worked in the kitchen like the legendary Tiny – real name Mary – Gallagher, who joined the club in 1967 and was following in the footsteps of her mother Lizzie Love and grandmother Maggie Lindsay, who had worked at Ibrox since the thirties. They were the heart and soul of Glasgow Rangers.

And groundsman Davie Roxburgh, who came to the club around the same time as me and who produced the Dynamo Kyiv pitch-shrinking magic!

The Rangers family was extensive, and it was loyal. They were fans who were on the payroll. And they did astonishing things for the club. Bob Reilly was the commercial manager, who was there long before me. He was old-school and would have done anything for the organization that was his life. Bob dealt with the sponsors and the kit deals we had and was very much the Rangers traditionalist. I am sure that as we started winning titles, his life became much easier. Nothing but the famous black socks with red tops would do, and he was another one who made me aware of the magnitude of Glasgow Rangers. He was the instigator of sponsorship on the strips. There were trails being blazed.

And then there was wee Doddie Soutar, who was the assistant kitman when I arrived. He was brought to the club by David Holmes, who knew him from the Lawrence Group. Doddie was from Govan and had a passion for the club all his life. When he started at Ibrox, he said, 'It feels as if I'm in heaven yet still alive.' He was some character, and just fabulous to have about the place. He loved the dressing room and the players loved him, and he could be trusted every inch of the way. What also made him special was that he was not in awe of the players – or the manager for that matter – and would not let them mess him about. He gave as good as he got. When we had trophy-winning pictures, I always made sure Doddie was in them. Clubs are not just about players. It is the whole operation.

Doddie was assistant to Jimmy Bell. Jimmy initially joined up with the club as driver of the team coach hired from Park's of Hamilton and he continued as kitman – at first combining the jobs – from my time all the way through to Giovanni van Bronckhorst in 2022. He passed away at the age of sixty-nine just before the Europa League semi-final. He was a huge supporter of the club and achieved iconic status with the fan base, and was much loved by various generations of players. And, just like Doddie, he would not let the players mess him about. He was given huge respect, something that escalated big time on a preseason trip to Il Ciocco in Italy.

We worked the players hard, but late in the afternoon I used to let them have an hour by the pool as the sun began to wane. Walter and I and all the players were relaxing when Jimmy suddenly got up, hitched up his Speedos and marched round to the diving board. He then climbed up the stairs, to the bemusement of a group of players and staff who watched in stunned silence as he eventually reached the springboard at the top.

Everyone had the same thought: 'Who are you kidding, Jimmy? You must be joking!'

But then he pulled up the budgie smugglers again and started bouncing on the board . . . before walking back along it once more. I think at that point we were all holding our collective breath in disbelief. Then he turned, ran to the front, a couple of bounces, and off he leapt into a flawless dive – let's say a jackknife with pike – and clean entry into the water. Had I been a judge, it would have been a perfect ten, and the audience to a man gave him a standing ovation.

Talk about unknown talents!

Meanwhile, Mo Johnston was not the only big-name player we signed in the summer of '89. Although, as a headline-maker, he will be king for ever more. Trevor Steven was someone I first saw when he was playing for Burnley against Liverpool at Turf Moor. He was an exceptionally talented midfielder and, although he was an England international player, he was from Berwick-upon-Tweed, which is as next door to Scotland as you can get.

Everton had paid Burnley £300,000 for his services, and in a curious twist Trevor had played for the then-Goodison Park club in the FA Cup final against Watford . . . who had featured Mo Johnston, our other headline signing that summer. And, incidentally, another future Rangers player, Andy Gray, scored in that game.

Walter and I travelled down to watch Everton play one midweek evening and we arranged to meet Trevor near their training ground at Bellefield – an area I knew well because I used to live near there – and we had a clandestine gathering at about eleven at night.

We sold the club to him and answered all his footballing questions, which led to us making a bid that was eventually taken to a tribunal to settle on a fee. Alan Montgomery, the Ibrox chief executive who had joined just a few months earlier from STV, where he had been a finance director, came to the tribunal with me. Eventually we were ordered to pay £1.525 million for Trevor, something that met with our appreciation. He was an England player, the right age and extraordinarily talented. And he had 299 Everton appearances under his belt. He was a wonderful piece of business.

Everton had other offers for him – including from

17. The trophy room at Ibrox. I made a fair contribution to the cause.

18. The best signing I ever made, Richard Gough. And it looks like I am letting him know it.

19. Getting ourselves into shape in Il Ciocco. Left to right, Davie Kirkwood, Terry Butcher, me, Davie Cooper and Ian Ferguson.

20. This is what it was all about. I show off the Championship trophy to the Ibrox support.

21. (*Above*) The most headlined signing in Scottish football. We unveil Mo Johnston at Ibrox.

22. (*Right*) My partner, my friend and my successor. The one and only Walter Smith.

23. Ally McCoist, as ever, trying to have the last word. Me, as ever, trying to make sure he doesn't get it.

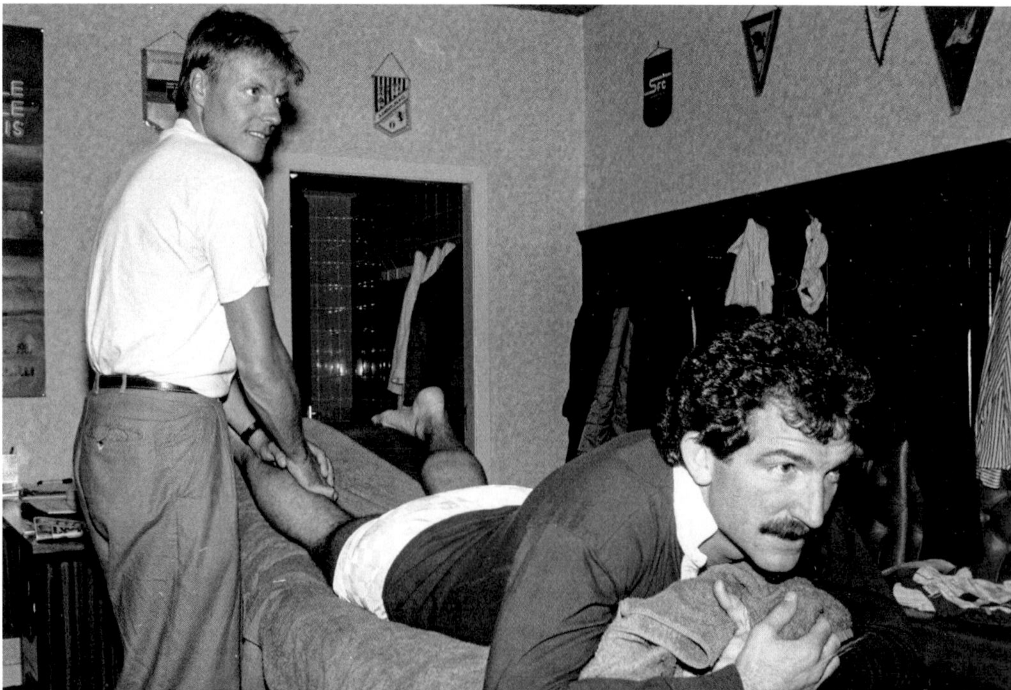

24. The beginning of the end of my playing career and a Dutch physio tries to salvage the issues with my calves.

25. The team behind the team. Phil and Walter flank the manager.

26. The *Rangers News* screams the headline that we signed the best right back in world . . .

27. . . . and here is Gary Stevens (on the right) with me and John Brown.

28. The courageous and talented Ian Durrant battles his way back after that horrific tackle by Neil Simpson. Walter and John McGregor lend moral support.

29. I'm clearly not happy about something. Looks like it might have been a goal lost to Celtic, but we got the upper hand on them over my time at Rangers.

30. (*Above*) Ol' Blue Eyes meets Ol' Blue Nose. I present Frank Sinatra with a decanter after he performed at the stadium.

31. (*Right*) And so, the end is near. David Murray announces my departure. And an astonishing era comes to its end.

Manchester United – but again, the temptation of European football (which was still banned for English clubs) was drawing him to us. It also meant that he could resume his partnership with his old pal Gary Stevens, who had come from Everton a year earlier and who was just brilliant for Rangers. Gary was an absolute athlete and was a wonderful attacking full back who went on to make 245 appearances for Rangers and outlasted me at the club. So too did Trevor . . . but therein lies a tale.

Later, when I had moved on to manage Liverpool, I got a call from Marseille informing me that they wanted to sign John Barnes. I was summoned to Paris to have a meeting with their infamous owner Bernard Tapie, who was many things, including politician, television host, actor and singer. His political career was full of legal battles and financial scandals, and eventually he was sentenced to prison.

At the time I was talking to Tapie, his club were in the middle of a five-in-a-row run of French championship triumphs, which would culminate in Marseille winning the 1993 Champions League, the inaugural edition of the competition that had formerly been the European Cup. However, that year he was accused of match-fixing involving his club and Valenciennes, and Marseille were eventually stripped of the French league title, although *not* the European crown.

The cheating scandal affected Rangers and haunted Walter for the rest of his days. It was a different Champions League set-up back then, but basically Rangers lost out to a place in the final by one goal. Walter's team had qualified for the competition's group stage – the first time it had been arranged that way – by beating Danish champions Lyngby and then Leeds United. They were then drawn to play CSKA Moscow, Club Brugge and Marseille. CSKA Moscow were beaten 6–0 at the Stade Vélodrome, Marseille's ground, amid allegations of spiked drinks, and the Russians' coach claiming that his players were 'got at' before suddenly changing his mind. Mark Hateley also revealed he had been offered money to miss Rangers' second game against the French side. Mark, as it turned out, was sent off in the previous game – a 2–1 win at Ibrox against Brugge – and always insisted that 'something had gone off there'. All of this dodgy business would become public once the scandal broke, but I'd already heard enough from people who I trusted, like Walter, that it came as no surprise to me.

Anyway, back to the Barnes story. I met Tapie in Paris, and he sent a driver to pick me up at the airport. This big, very fit Scandinavian-looking bloke ushered me to his car and, as soon as we were good to go, he reached under the seat and brought out a blue flashing light that he promptly placed on the roof of the car! And off we went, speeding through the Parisian traffic, ignoring the red lights.

When we got to Tapie's magnificent house, we pulled through these huge gates and into a massive courtyard. By the time we got to the front door, all his staff were lined up in black suits or waitress uniforms, waiting to greet me. If he was trying to impress me then he was doing an excellent job. It was a fabulous place, ornate and French Renaissance style.

So, over lunch, he tells me that he wants to buy Barnes and I say it is not happening because he is Liverpool's best player. He then asks – because he is in a hurry and only has about ninety minutes with me as he is going to his boat in Sardinia – who I can recommend. I suggested Trevor Steven, for whom you will recall Rangers had paid just over £1.5 million. Tapie subsequently paid £5.5 million for the player – at that time, the joint highest fee for a British player – thus turning a £4 million profit for us. Well, I say 'us', but by that time I was at Liverpool. I did not mind doing Rangers a favour, though. Not only that, but Trevor later returned to Ibrox after a single season, in which he won the French league, for just £2.2 million.

But that was still a long way off from my fourth year at Rangers. Back in the summer of '89 we were getting ready for the new season to start. I was very confident that we could go on to win the league because I always thought we had the best players.

We even enhanced the squad in November by bringing in Nigel Spackman from Queens Park Rangers. I loved him as a player. Nigel was the ultimate team man, who did not mind putting in the hard yards for his mates. He was the kind of midfielder who made sure that if he wasn't having the greatest of days then his immediate opponent would not be either. He'd had a spell at Liverpool, so I knew his background from sources there, and he was such a lovely fellow. Nigel actually only scored one goal for us that season, but he chose his moment well, to say the least!

It was in the fire and brimstone of the New Year derby against Celtic at Parkhead, the only goal of the game, and gave us our first Ne'erday league victory there in twenty-five years. If you are going to score one goal . . .

At no point was I nervous about how things would go. I knew we had a tight group of players, and we encouraged that no-one-likes-us-we-don't-care approach because we did feel like it was us against the rest.

It was a tough league back then in Scotland, and extremely competitive. Aberdeen and Hearts and Dundee United and Celtic were all strong teams. But in preseason in Italy and beyond, I could see we were bonding.

Mo was with us and he never lacked confidence in his

own ability. And it was justified. He made a slow start to his Rangers career, while all the headlines screamed around him, but I knew he would get going. Form is temporary but class is permanent and Mo Johnston was class. And in the 1989–90 season, with the wee man settled in just fine, and as we looked forward to Sinatra's visit and the Year of Culture, I knew I could borrow the lyrics from one of his most famous songs.

The Best Was Yet to Come . . .

10

The Apprentice

Mark Hateley. Now there was a good signing.

The first time I came across him was when we both played in Italy, me for Sampdoria, he as a striker for AC Milan. We played against one another, and we had a bit of chat on the pitch, but nothing socially away from it. I was an established and experienced player, and he was a few years younger, but I was taken with him. He was not the kind of bloke you would fancy playing against. He was big, athletic and fearless.

I remember a goal he scored in his first Milan derby against Inter, a good old-fashioned English centre forward's goal, a towering header at the far post. I was impressed and could see why an Italian giant like Milan had signed him. But at that time I hadn't really considered players I might want to take on as a manager because it had never really entered my thoughts that I would become one.

My time at Liverpool had come to an end in 1984 after

winning the European Cup final against Roma, a game in which I scored one of the shoot-out penalties, making it the last time I kicked a ball for the club. But I was still only thirty-one and at the peak of my game and had just enjoyed my best season ever in a Liverpool strip.

I had a major problem to address in terms of my future. My then-wife needed to live three years out of the country for tax reasons and Ken Bates, who owned Chelsea, made me an interesting offer. He said that if I signed for him, we could live in Guernsey for three days a week and I could come to London on Wednesday, Thursday and Friday to prepare for the match on Saturday. It was a plan that really intrigued me and seemed an inventive solution to the issues we had. I gave it a lot of thought.

Barcelona made me an offer too, but they would only make it a two-year deal when I wanted three. I was also asked if I fancied going to Roma to join up with Roberto Falcão and Toninho Cerezo, the Brazilian superstars who won the Scudetto in 1983. Falcão was rumoured to be the best-paid player in the world at the time. Back then, in Serie A, you could only have two foreign players in your side . . . so one of them would have had to go. But despite the Chelsea interest and suggestion, I knew that Italy was the place to be. All the best players in the world were heading there. And, of course, it was where I ended up . . . under curious circumstances.

Looking back, I am both surprised and disappointed that Liverpool did not come through with a Bates-style solution. Possibly the reason for that was the fact they were going to more than double the £352,000 they had paid for me seven years previously.

Liverpool finished the season as champions of England and Europe, as well as holders of the League Cup. After the open-top bus celebrations, we went to what was then Swaziland – now Eswatini – to play two games against Spurs, who had won the UEFA Cup. The competition we were there for was called – snazzy title – the Royal Swazi Sun's Soccer Challenge Floating Trophy, and it was played over two legs. I played in neither of them despite travelling all that way.

Before the first game, I had been partying on the flights from Liverpool to London and from London to Durban in South Africa. Remember: we had just won the European Cup. When we arrived, we then joined up with the Spurs players and got involved in their shenanigans. The captain of Spurs was my old mate Steve Perryman, with whom I had been a youth player at White Hart Lane. Anyone who knows me will vouch for the fact that I am a hopeless drinker. I was rooming with Kenny Dalglish, woke in the morning, and told Kenny that I felt terrible. Kenny went to tell our manager, Joe Fagan, and Joe came to the room to look at me, tried to speak to me and, after my response, said: 'Oh, we can do without him!' Kenny played in my position in midfield and it seemed I was a long way from sorely missed. We won 5–2. Joe was right.

The day after the game, we chartered two small planes to take us down to Durban for a few days on the beach, and we asked some of the Spurs boys to join us. They declined because they were going to Sun City, but their black players did not want to do the trip because apartheid was still in operation, and not wanting to be treated like second-class citizens – which would have been hellish – they stayed in Swaziland.

While I was in Durban, I got a call from Liverpool saying that they had agreed a fee with Sampdoria. So I flew from Durban to London and from London to Genoa and missed the second leg against Spurs. When I got to Genoa, I was met by Sampdoria's president, Paolo Mantovani – a fine man – who was there on the tarmac to greet me. I jumped into his limousine straight from the plane. I was whisked through the airport with no customs, security or passport checks, and taken to the club's offices in one of the main streets of Genoa. It was there I was to negotiate a deal.

There were maybe about 2,000 fans gathered outside waiting for news, and there was a balcony on to which Paolo eventually went to signal to the supporters: 'Not yet, not yet!' I knew then that I was in a strong negotiating position. With the crowd outside, he had to go a bit further than he was hoping to in our talks. And so I started another wonderful phase of my life.

Playing in Italy was so much easier than in England. Every game was warfare at Liverpool because, for the opposition, playing us was a cup final. We had to battle for twenty minutes before the game would settle and then, of course, our better players would take over. I'd experience the same thing when I was at Rangers.

Italy was different for midfield players. It was more straightforward. Teams would drop off and there was no instant high press for us to deal with, although of course it was harder for strikers, because their workplace would get a bit crowded. This allowed midfielders to get their heads up and, if you could make a pass, it was a dream to play in.

I loved it and I honestly thought I could easily squeeze another couple of years on to my playing career. I was planning to stay for the third year of my contract and had told the president I would do so . . . but that was before Rangers came calling. As it happens, I let Paolo down a bit because I said I would stay and, on the back of that, he agreed to sell Gianfranco Matteoli to Inter Milan at the end of the season. He told me that had he known I was leaving then he would never have entered that deal. Matteoli was a six-times-capped Italian who played for several clubs in Serie A and would have been expendable had I stayed. But it did not work out that way and I should really apologize to Paolo.

And, in the end, I did not get to play in my final home game for Sampdoria because I had the flu. I suspect the supporters felt I was at it before going to Rangers, but I was genuinely ill and I would have loved the opportunity to say *arrivederci*. They were a great club and group of fans. It was just the most wonderful two years for me.

While all this was happening, the aforementioned Mark Hateley was making his own successful way in life and was now a genuine star at AC Milan. That was why, in my first season at Ibrox, I tried to sign him, employing the well-tested route of using a football writer to tap him up. On this occasion, it was my co-author on this book.

Chick Young was working for the *Evening Times* in Glasgow, which back then was an influential publication. He used to phone me early – before training – to see if he could eke a story out of me. So, one morning, I suggested to him that he might want to hint that we were interested in Hateley. The bold reporter replied that it would be good if he could have a word with Mark, but added that he didn't have this number. After all, these were pre-mobile days.

'You might want to write this one down,' I said, and gave him Mark's home number in Milan. I will let my co-author take up the story.

Mark was charming. I explained who I was and why I was calling and told him that I had a contact who had suggested that he might be considering a move to Rangers. He was great and said all the right things about moving to Rangers and how attractive the idea was . . . but that he had an offer from Monaco and he had to decide where to go next. I repeat . . . Monaco.

It was, I think January, and it was about eight in the morning, and I looked outside the window of my newspaper offices on Albion Street in Glasgow. It was still dark and the rain was sheeting it down. And then I thought of Monte Carlo. The French Riviera and that glorious climate. And I said: 'Are you mental? Monaco or Glasgow? Give me a break.' And I might have hung up.

I might have then told Graeme that it went well.

So Hateley did go to Monaco, but what happened next is next door to unbelievable.

At the 1990 World Cup, Scotland played two games at the Luigi Ferraris Stadium, home to Sampdoria, and me, chairman David Murray and director Ian Skelly were staying in Monaco, just a couple of hours' drive back up the Med coastline from Genoa. I remember that, as you do, David had his Rolls-Royce driven down to Monte Carlo.

Anyway, one morning I went for a walk, and who should I meet but Mark Hateley taking his kids for an ice cream. So I just chanced my arm and asked him if he fancied coming to Rangers. And he simply said, 'I'll let you know.' The next morning, there was an envelope left for me at reception at the Hôtel de Paris, where we were staying, and inside it was a note that simply said: 'I'm in.' There was also a number, which Mark asked me to phone. It was that of his agent, Dennis Roach.

Mark agreed to come to Scotland for a fraction of what he was earning in Monaco. I can tell you the exact fraction . . . one-tenth of what he was getting there, owing to the fact it was tax-free where he was. That is how much he wanted to come to Rangers. It was so crazy that I still laugh at the insanity of it all.

But come he did . . . and the financial situation got worse for him. For the first three months of his employment at Ibrox, it turned out that for some strange reason we were paying his wages to an apprentice at the club, who never returned any of it and spent every penny. I have no recollection of his identity, but if you are reading this and it was you – and you'll be in your fifties now – then you owe Glasgow Rangers a right few bob! I am sure the lad did not ever make it to the big time, but with all that money in his pocket the kid probably didn't care.

Hateley turned out to be a brilliant signing for Rangers. There was never a need to light a firecracker under him. He was a top professional and he formed a great partnership with Ally McCoist in a team who were bonding as a fabulous group of guys. McCoist – along with Ian Durrant – was the heart and soul of the dressing room banter, which was as ferocious as ever. I often wondered why big Terry Butcher didn't just banjo them. Alistair was the joint-best presence in a dressing room I have ever seen . . . or heard, more likely. It was fabulous at Anfield with the Liverpool lads, but Ibrox topped it for banter, and Coisty had his match in Ray Wilkins.

Razor was a wonderful human being. He contributed as much to our team in the dressing room as he did on the park. He played his last game for Rangers in November 1989 in a 3–0 win over Dunfermline, two years after joining us in a £250,000 deal from Paris Saint-Germain. In that time, he played ninety-five games, scored four goals, and won two championships and one League Cup. I will never forget his volley against Celtic from outside the box in August 1988, right in front of their fans in the Broomloan Road end at Ibrox.

But what a diamond of a man. I seemed to have played against him all my career, both of us as central midfielders, him at Chelsea, Manchester United and AC Milan, me at Liverpool and Sampdoria. We had a fair old rivalry, even though Ray was not a physical type of player. I remember in training one day I was playing for the English side in our fives, and I went for a ball about four feet off the ground. Neale Cooper – another good lad we had signed – launched a tackle and caught me square in the ribcage with his knee. And we were both on the same side!

As it happened, I had broken three ribs and was lying on the ground struggling to breathe. I looked up to see all the concerned faces of the players gathered round me, some just laughing. And then Razor broke into the circle and said: 'Let me in, let me in. I have waited ten years to see this bastard like this.' I wanted to laugh but the pain was too much. He was a wonderful human being and had his own Cockney banter that lit up the place. He was a very funny man and a delight to be around. I still think about him a lot.

I think he played the best football of his career at Rangers, despite criticism in his early days about always playing the ball sideways. The pitches were crap back then and players needed an extra touch. Ray just did not want to give the ball away.

And what an asset in the changing room. Not long after he signed, he would occasionally come in wearing a wig – he had a couple – and played it deadpan. The boys did not know whether to say anything, whether he was joking or not, and Razor just kept it straight. He was brilliant. It was hysterical. I remember Walter coming up to me and saying that Razor was in the dressing room wearing a wig. Was that something he sometimes did, or was he taking the piss? I said that I had no effin' idea!

I could not believe that we managed to sign Ray. He could not get into the team at PSG, and his agent Dennis Roach had suggested we could get him for around a quarter of a million. We flew in a private plane to a small airport in Paris and I went to negotiate. The talks went on and on. The pilot of our plane then said we would not get out that night because the airport closed at midnight. So he had to fly the aircraft about five minutes away to Charles de Gaulle, which was open twenty-four hours, and await us there! Eventually we got the deal done and Razor flew back to Glasgow with us in time to make his debut the next day, 28 November 1987, in a 3–2 win over Hearts at Ibrox.

He played twenty-nine games that season, but the next one – when he scored that volley against Celtic when it was 1–1 and we went on to win 5–1 – was the autumn, winter and spring that he won a place in the hearts of the Rangers support. They absolutely loved him. It was impossible not to.

Ray only played two seasons in Glasgow because his family wanted him to return to London, and so he took the chance to go to Queens Park Rangers, but his impact was such that he was later inducted into the Rangers Hall of Fame. I'll never forget him and what he did for us. He was up there with Terry Butcher and Richard Gough in terms of what he contributed to the dressing room, but he was also the consummate professional and such a nice little fellow. You do not play eighty-four times for England without being something special, and Razor sure was that. When Walter succeeded me as manager, he thought about asking Ray to become his assistant, but he declined the offer to return north. He passed away in 2018, aged just sixty-one. It was heartbreaking.

So too was what happened to Neale Cooper. Tattie – as he was known to all and sundry – joined us in 1988 from Aston Villa, but of course he had made his name with Aberdeen as a member of their European Cup Winners' Cup-winning team in 1983. He won two titles and a League Cup at Rangers and was full of fun. That said, I did not see the funny side of him the day he smashed my ribs, although his own Ibrox career was restricted by a series of injuries. He was a lovely lad and was wonderful in the dressing room. Like Ray Wilkins, he passed away in 2018. Tattie was only fifty-four.

Teamwork and camaraderie are massive requirements in a football club. In my five years at Rangers, I met some fantastic characters. Valuable players are not always huge personalities, but the ones I had did have everything. I used to tell them that I would only find out what sort of character they really had when the going got tough – and boy, did I have some real men in that dressing room.

That restaurant in Glasgow's West End at Kelvinbridge, La Parmigiana – which I had first been told about by Trevor Francis, who loved his Italian food – became my favourite Glasgow watering hole. Eventually we ended up taking the whole team there of an afternoon, as the management at La Parmigiana would close it to the public and the whole first-team squad of Rangers would have a session, eating and drinking. Someone came up with the phrase that the team that drinks together wins together, but I preferred to refer to it as bonding. Either way, it seemed to work and I know Walter Smith continued the tradition after I left.

In my Rangers days, the height of my socializing was a fine meal and a glass of wine. I have always appreciated decent food. Glasgow is a place where you can find trouble if you want it, or even if you do not, but I never did. I am proud that I never got into any bother in that sense in all my time at Rangers. It helped that I always had my wits about me.

As well as being the first player-manager of Rangers, I was also the first man to serve as manager and director simultaneously since the legendary Bill Struth, who was involved in a boardroom coup in the late forties. There was no coup required with me. By the time David Murray was chairman I had become the second-largest shareholder, and he asked me to join the board. But I only lasted ten minutes at board meetings before I got . . . well, bored.

David and I had that agreement from day one, that he would run the business and he would not interfere in the football side, although of course he could not stop offering his opinion. Between us two there was no need for specially arranged bonding, such as at La Parmigiana with the players, because we would have an early supper four or five times a week at Ristorante Raffaelli in Edinburgh, maybe from 6 to 7.30 p.m., and then go home. We had a fantastic relationship.

But while I'm discussing club legends, there is another guy I need to talk about. Phil Boersma was my buddy from the first day we met as young men at Middlesbrough. Eventually I took him everywhere I went as a manager – with the exception of Torino, but we did go to Ibrox, Liverpool, Galatasaray, Benfica and Blackburn. Jack Charlton had paid £75,000 for him, and although he is a couple of years older than me, we hit it off at once. He was a loyal friend and a fabulous fitness coach with a real football knowledge learned from people like Bill Shankly and the other managers at Liverpool who coached him. Phil played a huge part in getting me my move from Teesside to Anfield.

This is how it worked. There was a guy in Liverpool called Bob Rawcliffe who owned the Wheatsheaf Garage in the Knotty Ash area. Bob Paisley would go there every morning to pick his horses, and the other Bob would put his bets on for him. The lad who owned the garage was a friend of Phil's. So there was an information conduit from Bob Paisley to the other Bob to Phil to me and all down the line. Although Middlesbrough did not realize it, I was up to speed with Liverpool's progress in trying to sign me.

From day one, Phil was a magnificent friend and he was good at his job. I had no hesitation in bringing him to Ibrox. And he adored it.

No one was let off lightly in their jobs at Rangers. Not Phil and not even me. Every preseason, I would have a calf issue, which we later realized was to do with me not stretching it properly in the summer weeks off. I had an operation and then Phil's idea of me building up the muscle had me walking and running up the stairs in the main stand of the stadium twenty times . . . with him on my back.

He loved the players at Rangers, and they loved and respected him because of his fitness levels, which were higher than those of the first team. Even at forty, he could outrun them all, except for Richard Gough, and he was also not averse to a night out with them. And when he did, his lips would be sealed. He never told me anything about what happened on the town. However, to this day, he thinks I do not know he used to go on nights out with them.

He and Walter both lived in Helensburgh and were as thick as thieves. They shared a schoolboy sense of humour. Phil was just a lovely, down-to-earth bloke. And as the fitness coach, he played a huge part in the recuperation of Ian Durrant after his horror injury. Phil was a bit of an unsung hero at Rangers.

My years at Rangers really were the most incredible times. I was surrounded by the most wonderful people, like dear Doc Cruickshank. Donald was like my wise uncle, and I saw him as a mentor. He knew how to slow me down. He had such a lovely way of 'suggesting' that I might want to do something a certain way, telling me off really. Nine times out of ten I followed his advice. The whole period of my life at Rangers was just a script for a movie. I learned so much about other people and myself. There was such a sense of family about the club at the time. There was a special warmth.

Looking back, I was too aggressive, too harsh and too ready to confront people, and that was a failing in me. But I walked into the job with no training in how to handle players or the media and I had to learn on the job. Every day was a school day at Ibrox. If I had my time there again, I think I could have done things a bit differently. Maybe I could have been more understanding of certain players who didn't show the same passion or disappointment as I did when we lost a game. I was never on a coaching course until I had finished with management, at which point I thought I would go on one just to see what I had missed. So it was three days on a residential course in Warwickshire in the Midlands. The only thing I took away was the word 'revisit', in the sense that you must keep repeating your message to your players until it registers.

But that was the very opposite of what it was like at Liverpool, where we were told once.

Ronnie Moran and Joe Fagan would say that if they had to tell you something a second time, 'It means one thing, son: you're not a Liverpool player and you won't be here very long.' I am delighted to say I never had that said to me. What I did have behind me was the fact that I had learned at the Oxbridge of coaching, a place where legends lectured. If you do not listen to Bob Paisley and Joe Fagan and Ronnie Moran, then you have no chance.

And Jock Stein. A real football giant. They used to say that when Big Jock came out to play, the foxes headed for the woods. He was always one step ahead of the game. In 1983 I was on a Liverpool tour to Bangkok and Hong Kong, but the Scotland manager told me that as captain

I should be with the national squad on a tour of Canada. I only agreed to join them if the SFA got me a first-class ticket from Bangkok via Tokyo to Vancouver. So I flew all the way from East Asia across the Pacific to Vancouver on the West Coast of North America to join up with the squad. Normally, I would be rooming with Kenny Dalglish, but he was not on the trip. Jock told me I would be sharing with Charlie Nicholas, who was on red-hot form with Celtic at the time and was wanted by the big clubs down south. Then I worked it out. Jock and Bob Paisley were big pals and my job was to tap up Charlie to come to Anfield. I eventually worked out their masterplan! But clearly I failed, as he signed for Arsenal. Should have come to Liverpool, though: he would have had a better career.

11

Ten Men Went to Mo . . .

Mo Johnston was never going to be properly accepted by some of the Rangers fans until he scored against Celtic. At first he was talked about as 'not doing this and not doing that'. Strikers and goalkeepers are much more likely to have statistics thrown at them because it's more straightforward to do it for them than it is for other positions, but it is never as obvious as that. I've had a lifetime in football and I see it differently. Mentality is so important and Mo had a special one. I knew he would win those fans over.

He did this by scoring the only goal of the game against his old club Celtic at Ibrox on 4 November 1989. For some sections of the home support, who had struggled with his signing, it was time to think again. Now they saw that he was the real deal. Although the teammates who ran to celebrate with him already knew his worth. They all knew his talent because they witnessed it daily in training.

But I was never in doubt, even during what some might have seen as our slow start to the season, in which we had two defeats and one draw in our first three games. In fact, we won only two of our first eight games and scored just six goals. Maurice scored his first for the club in a 1–0 win over Aberdeen in September but, all these years on, I have no recollection of worrying. At no time did I think to myself, 'Bloody hell.' I knew Mo Johnston was a top goal-scorer, I had played with him in the national team, and I knew his fitness levels, work rate and desire to do well.

On our way to the title, we won seven games with a 1–0 scoreline, and time after time it was a goal by our new striker that made the difference. We were defensively watertight, and if you have someone up front who can sniff out one chance for you then you are on your way.

He was different from McCoist, who had a fantastic instinct for being in the right place at the right time. McCoist was lucky at times . . . but all those goals could not be down to luck all the time. That said, maybe Ally could have run the channels a bit more, and run the hard yards when we did not have possession.

Before Mo's goal against Celtic, we even went out of the European Cup in the first round, losing to Bayern Munich 3–1 at Ibrox and managing a 0–0 draw in Bavaria, where I got abuse from the media for what they thought was a defensive performance. It is called counterattacking football, and I was hoping we might have nicked a goal from a set-piece. It was no disgrace losing to Bayern. They were a wonderful team representing a great club with massive resources and a superb infrastructure. They were and still are the richest and most successful outfit in Germany by a country mile.

European exit in the first round, seemingly toiling in the league, it looked bad at the start . . . and yet I was never fazed. I honestly felt that we had navigated the correct course. We had spent a lot of money – Mo Johnston, Trevor Steven, Davie Dodds, Nigel Spackman came in – but we also sold a few players. And even with Davie Cooper, Kevin Drinkell and Razor Wilkins moving on, we had a strong squad. It was all about balance.

I was keeping a lot of journalists in a job, but the usefulness was one-way. There was not a lot of warmth coming back to us. My whole football education had previously been to play it down, but I wasn't happy with the reaction. They were on top of us at the slightest opportunity. They seldom saw the bigger picture and the headlines often hammered us.

I was by now cynical, mistrusting and more likely to have a go. Scotland can be a place of parochial attitudes and there is an ingrained thing about not wanting people to be successful. The SFA and STV went out of their way to make life difficult for us.

And, to be honest, I felt there was a sectarian divide in the media. There were a lot of organizations and people properly after us. David Murray and Walter Smith shared my thoughts, and David was right up for the no-one-likes-us-we-don't-care approach.

I had travelled a long way in football, and I had enjoyed being successful. It was a feeling I relished. Winning and being top of the tree was way better than the alternative, and I never envisaged it ending. So when I saw that people were jealous of us, I was never in a conciliatory mood. If they wanted a fight, I was right up for it. We had to win the league – that was the priority above everything else – and I was determined we would, despite the desires of some of the more biased media and any injuries we might sustain.

We could not win either of the domestic cups that season. In the League Cup, we beat Arbroath, Morton, Hamilton and Dunfermline, before meeting Aberdeen in the final at Hampden for the third season in succession. Paul Mason gave Aberdeen – now managed by Alex Smith and Jocky Scott – the lead before Mark Walters equalized from the penalty spot. But a second goal from Mason in extra time meant that we lost to them for the first time in the trio of finals.

I never won the main domestic cup competition as a player north or south of the border – although I did with Sampdoria in Italy and managed Liverpool to joy at Wembley. And we didn't last too long in the tournament with Rangers that season. We beat St Johnstone but then drew Celtic in the fourth round and lost 1–0 at Parkhead.

For us the league championship was the priority above everything. During this season, it became very clear I was coming towards the end of my playing career. I had the problem with my calf that, had I stayed on in Italy, I could have managed for another couple of seasons. But I would have finished there, as I had no interest in slipping down the leagues. I was still very fit, but the calf problem was down to lack of knowledge at the time. I should have been constantly stretching my Achilles when I was sunning myself on my month's holiday on the beach in Majorca. There was an operation to undergo, but it didn't work.

Professionals need to remember why they are playing in the first place, that sheer joy you felt as a kid when you kicked a ball with your mates. The greatest sport on earth. Nothing lasts for ever and I would recommend that players keep going as long as they can. I knew I had been lucky. No bad injuries, mostly because of luck, but also because I looked after myself, as I still do even now. But I was coming to the end, and I had one last appearance to make for Rangers that season.

I picked myself as substitute in a game against Dunfermline at Ibrox, which we won 2–0, the final fixture of the season. I was fit, right enough, but not match fit. That is a different thing. And there is a big difference. So I put myself on with just twenty minutes to go. What I did not know was that the players had agreed not to pass the ball to me – a plot hatched by that bugger Wilkins, apparently – and I could not understand at first what was happening. I would show for it time and time again, but the ball never came. And then it dawned on me. It took me five minutes to realize that the players were all giggling and taking the piss. However, I sorted it. When there was a stoppage in the game, I told them that if they didn't start passing it to me they would be in the following day – Sunday or not – for eight in the morning. Oh yes, the power of your position!

But the title was already ours by then. With six games left, we had been five points ahead of Aberdeen, and we cruised from there, beating Celtic 3–0 on April Fool's Day. We then drew with Aberdeen and beat Motherwell before wrapping it all up at Tannadice three weeks later, with our nineteenth clean sheet of the campaign in a 2–0 win over Dundee United, with goals from Stuart Munro – I repeat, Stuart Munro – and Trevor Steven. That made it two championships in a row.

However, it was a time of change. David Murray had appointed a finance director called Alan Montgomery, who had come from STV where he was director of finance and administration. That is the same STV who had stitched me up over the touchline ban. One of Montgomery's jobs was to provide more cash for me to use in the transfer market. It did not work out, because we did not see eye to eye. He wanted a bigger say in what I saw as my side of the club – the football – and although the chairman thought he would be an asset, it was clear to me that I could not work with him.

Montgomery started wearing club tracksuits, coming to training and overstepping the line. He may have had expertise in one area, but suddenly he was putting out corner flags and getting caught up in things that were not in his remit. I told David as much and, after lasting just eight months in the job, Montgomery went to work in one of the Murray media companies. I did not miss him.

So, by the end of the season, the playing days were over. I do not remember being that sad about hanging up my boots but rather a feeling of being quietly chuffed about everything I had achieved with my clubs and country, and the fact that I had played in three World Cups. I was not emotional about it at all, just proud that I had achieved what I'd set out to do. And now I was a full-time manager.

It's not for me to make judgements on what my legacy at Rangers was or how people will regard what I did in forty years' time, but I'm proud of what happened. It really was an incredible time at the club and I was always convinced we would win the league in 1989–90. We had the right squad, and Mo as a player – never mind everything else around him – was the icing on the cake.

It is strange because my memory tells me that I was 100 per cent sure we would go on to be champions and yet we lost our first two games, to St Mirren and Hibs, and drew with Celtic. One point from three games would normally have our critics dusting down the crisis headlines. But I could feel us gelling together as the season went on. Mo's first goal came in early September, a header on the end of a cross from Trevor Steven against Aberdeen at Ibrox.

We were beginning to justify my confidence by November, when we went top, and I knew we would finish the season there. Football is not a complicated game, and we had a winning system. Pitches were not of the same quality that they are now, and I did not want my goalkeeper continually rolling the ball out to play along the back line. You do not take chances on bumpy surfaces and, in any case, deep down, defenders do not want to be overpassing it near the goal, because one misplaced pass can lead to you conceding. I would rather the goalie got a throw or a pass that took out the front line of the opposition and got the ball moving forward.

And while we had played 4–4–2 at Liverpool, I could see the advantages of a three at the back, which becomes five when you have to defend and are out of possession.

But the basic philosophy is that the rest of us – myself included – are hod carriers, labourers, only there to serve the badge-kissers, the strikers. You know, the boys who like a bit of glory hunting. The ones who run to the crowd. We are only there to find them a bit of time and space.

They talk now about attacking wing backs as if they have just been invented, but I wanted my full backs to get forward then. Don't forget that I was part of a Liverpool team in which full backs scored from open play in two of the three European Cup finals in which I played.

But I set the team up according to the players we had. I was not going to ask players to play out of position and do something they were not capable of. It would be insane to sign players like Terry Butcher, Richard Gough and Graham Roberts, and then play them outside their natural habitat. They were the rocks on which we built our side. Ian Durrant was a natural box-to-box player with a massive talent and engine, and the only thing I had to tell him was to make sure he got back as quickly as he got forward.

You must know your players. I used to sit them down at the start of the season and tell them that footballers came in three groups: A, B and C. I explained that Group A only needed telling something once, B needed reminding once a month, and that C were the dummies who needed to be told every day, and even then it would not register. I would then ask them: 'Who is in Group A?' And of course they all put their hands up. However, it was my experience that plenty were C material. I'd then say: 'We'll soon fuckin' find out, won't we?' It was a humorous way of delivering a serious message.

It was hard making decisions about players, but it had to be done. When I came in, I thought Cammy Fraser, Dougie Bell and Bobby Russell were all good players and maybe a bit unlucky not to be kept on, but I had made up my mind that I wanted different types. Bobby in particular, like Davie Cooper, enjoyed a rebirth of his career at Motherwell, where he played 131 games and was, alongside Coop, part of their Scottish Cup-winning team.

And there was Ted McMinn, who definitely fell into the unpredictable category. The opposition had no chance of knowing what he was going to do next because he didn't either. I liked him, but nothing I told him seemed to register. Ted – real name Kevin – was some character. He had been signed by Jock Wallace from Queen of the South for £100,000 and the fans loved his unpredictable style. He scored the winner in the 1986–87 League Cup semi-final against Dundee United and helped win the final against Celtic. He eventually teamed up with Jock again, in Seville.

I remember he was touch-and-go for a game because

of an injury, and it was a late fitness test. So I told the coaching staff to delay it until some of the crowd were in the stadium, because although he doubted his fitness I knew he would respond to the fans. And he did. And he played in the game.

I mentioned before that the first big-name player I let go was Derek Johnstone, who had been a Scotland teammate. He was a great character, but I just felt that his best days were behind him. The morning I decided to tell him, I woke in my dad's house worrying about facing him, but then I realized it was part of the job, that I was a manager now and that I had been hired by the directors because they trusted my judgement. Going forward, I had to learn that releasing players could not be a problem for me if we wanted to go on to better things.

Of all the players I let go over the five years there was maybe only one regret . . . Davie Cooper. Although he insisted on it when I told him I could not guarantee him an automatic starting place. It was only years later I thought about him playing just off the centre forward, a position he might have been made for, but the moment had long gone. I do not know why it didn't occur to me at the time. He was special and his statistics back that up: seventy-five goals in 540 appearances for Rangers. Anyway, Coop had long departed from Ibrox by the time we won the 1989–90 title.

Beating Celtic was the key because it gives you such a psychological boost as well as the two points, *and* you deny them any. A league campaign is a slog, so mentality is really important and we were strong in that department. Once you have won a championship, you get the taste for it, and that is why I was so furious about blowing it in 1987–88.

But by the summer of 1990, Sinatra was crooning in Govan, the title was won and my playing days were ended. My time cleaning my own boots – and I still did sometimes – was up, and playing had become second to being a manager. Incidentally, I have a bit of a phobia about shoes. I am constantly brushing them and never wear a pair out, preferring instead to buy new ones all the time. Ironically, in eight managerial jobs, I only got the boot three times!

For me, the combination of playing and managing had become impossible. I felt I could no longer train, stay fit *and* pursue managerial duties. I was never off planes, always flying up and down the country to watch players who were recommended to us, and then either ending our interest or going back to watch them again.

It would be unimaginable nowadays to be a player-manager at a top club. I was doing everything back then. I was super busy. These days, there are too many media duties and demands on your time to play for and manage a club. Looking back, I cannot believe I did juggle the jobs for so long. At the age of thirty-five, I had loved the cut and thrust of it all and the concept of being sacked one day never even entered my mind. In any case, if it ever came to that, they would not need to bin me; I would have walked. Probably in brand-new shoes.

As the 1990–91 season dawned – which, although I did not know it then, was to be my final one at Ibrox – I was still on the hunt for talent. And you never know how you are going to stumble upon it.

At the draw for the European Cup, I got talking to the agent of the Dutch left winger Pieter Huistra, who was at Twente Enschede at the time. The agent said that he was looking for a club, and despite an offer from PSV Eindhoven would love to move abroad.

I said we would need to look at him in training, so he came initially to our training camp in Italy at Il Ciocco, and then to Glasgow, where he eventually played in a friendly against Queen's Park at Lesser Hampden. I liked him and we agreed to pay Twente £500,000, which was about £300,000 less than PSV bid, but there was some complicated rule in the Netherlands at the time that allowed him to go abroad for a fixed fee. Maybe Twente just did not want him playing against them. He became the first Dutch player to play for Rangers – although plenty followed over the next decade and more – and he eventually played his part in five championships, two Scottish Cup and three League Cup wins.

But I loved what he said after his time at Ibrox ended:

> Communication was not a problem because I spoke English. Mind you, Scottish was a bit different. It really did take quite a while until I was able to understand some of our players.
>
> But once I could understand Ian Durrant and Ian Ferguson, I was fine. Seriously though, I felt at home right from the beginning, and I knew I had made the right choice.

Yes, there is English and then there is the Glaswegian of the dressing room.

Pieter was a late one into Rangers, in terms of my career there, but my final signing was Brian Reid from Morton. Unfortunately, the big centre half suffered a cruciate ligament injury shortly after coming to us and that limited his appearances.

Players loved it with us and one of those was Ben-Zion Shabbtai Ginzburg – 'Boni' to you and me – the Israeli national keeper, whom we bought from Beitar Jerusalem. He was such a lovely fellow. Although he played sixty-eight times for Israel, he had to come to us as back-up to Chris Woods. Boni managed just a handful of first-team games, but one of them was vital and he was brilliant. He played in the first Old Firm game of the 1989–90 season at Parkhead and produced a terrific performance in the 1–1 draw. As it turned out, that was the only point Celtic took from us all term. I seem to recall that one of the reasons Boni had to return to Israel was to complete his national service.

Boni became the first Israeli goalkeeper to play in Europe when he signed for us, but he was not the only Israeli player I acquired. I had known Avi Cohen from his time at Liverpool – after he left Anfield he went home to play for Maccabi Tel Aviv. But I knew his character and ability, and I brought him to Ibrox in 1987. He was incredibly popular in the dressing room. Tragedy struck in December 2010 when he was seriously injured in a motorbike accident and later died in hospital. I was terribly affected by that. He was such a genuine and likeable man.

We have lost too many good guys way too young over the years.

12

One for the Road

As I've mentioned before, I'm a lightweight when it comes to the booze. But every now and then you have to swallow more than your pride when it comes to helping your club.

I was a huge admirer of Oleh Kuznetsov and made an inquiry to agent and friend Pini Zahavi – another Israeli – as to whether Dynamo Kyiv would be willing to sell him. Kuznetsov was a magnificent defender and captain of what was then the USSR, although he was also skipper of the interim CIS after the Soviet Union collapsed *and* of the independent Ukraine!

Pini indicated that they would be prepared to take the money, and we agreed a fee of £1.2 million. However, this involved a deputation of no fewer than ten men from the club coming to Glasgow to negotiate the deal, so I decided to take them all to La Parmigiana. Incidentally, it is now under new ownership and has a different name but I have been back and it is still lovely.

I learned these visiting chaps had a liking for a certain cognac and so I made sure the owner had stacks of bottles of it for their visit. A case, I think.

But I have never seen anyone sink drink like these gentlemen. And they insisted I toast our negotiations with them at what seemed thirty-second intervals. The words *za zdorovye* – Russian for 'cheers' – echoed in my head all night. 'We must drink to deal!' Which we did. And again. And again. And again. There was a case of the stuff and yet the owner of the restaurant had to send out one of his staff to comb other eateries nearby to get another half a dozen bottles. It was insane. I couldn't get out of my bed for the next twenty-four hours, and to this very day it is still the drunkest I have ever been in my life. But it worked and we got him.

Oleh made his debut in a 5–0 whipping of St Mirren and looked sensational. He rattled the post with a thirty-yard drive that was hit so hard it rebounded almost to the halfway line. I thought to myself: 'We've signed something special here.' He had actually played in the Dynamo Kyiv team we put out of the European Cup when we narrowed the pitch, but I do not remember bringing that up when he signed for us. And he became the stuff of legend in Glasgow.

Satty Singh is a city Indian restaurateur and a big Rangers fan. When his son was born, he swore he would name him after the next player to score a goal for the club, confident that it would be Ally McCoist or Mark Hateley. But it was Kuznetsov! And the irony is that it was his only goal for the club in thirty-five matches over four years. Oleg Singh is now an adult and, by all accounts, a thoroughly nice chap, and still involved in his dad's curry house. Incidentally, Oleg's brother is named after Mark Walters.

Tragically, it all went wrong for the other Oleh. He ruptured his cruciate ligament in just his second game – against St Johnstone in Perth – and was out for a year. He played some other matches but was a shadow of the player we signed.

That McDiarmid Park fixture was played on 20 October 1990. Kuznetsov's arrival had been held up until the end of the Soviet season, although he had played for Dynamo in a preseason friendly at Ibrox in which he was magnificent. We had lost that game 3–1. Little did I know it then, but the incident at Perth lit the blue touchpaper that would eventually set off the explosion that saw me walking out on the club. I was unhappy at the tackle that floored Oleh and furious that we had dropped points. He had incurred a serious injury, which was clearly career-threatening.

In the dressing room after the match, I was in a full rage and ranting at everyone, and then a woman called

Aggie Moffat – she was the tea lady at McDiarmid Park – came in at the end and complained about the state of the changing area, saying that the players had knocked the mud off their boots. They had, but we had swept it into a corner. Still, she was going nuts. I remember asking her what she wanted me to do with it, take it back to Ibrox? Voices were raised and I probably didn't cover myself in glory. Looking back, I was probably guilty of raising my voice, but I had just watched my £1 million player suffer a career-threatening injury!

But the rumblings of discontent had begun. I left the ground and began to reflect about what was going on . . .

I have to emphasize that all the issues were coming from outside the club. I felt we were still moving forward and that the group was strong. I never felt anything but support from the chairman and the board. We had done the hard part, dragging Rangers back into the modern football world, and were making inroads into European football. I knew I did not have to be critical of my players because the experienced pros were hard enough on themselves when things did go wrong. The English players came into the club and fed off the passion of the fans. And once you have that bond, it is hard to break.

The club had moved to such a place that major agents were calling to offer Rangers their big-name players. We had come a long way. Inside Ibrox I felt extremely comfortable. There was a special chemistry all around and no players ever took liberties with members of staff. There was a genuine feeling that we were all in this together. In that sense everything was just tickety-boo. Ibrox was a happy home.

And yet something was gnawing at me. The papers had me on their back and front pages daily, thereby increasing their sales off the back of Rangers, and I was uncomfortable with that. I had become the stick with which they could batter the club.

The Aggie aggro had lit a fuse, but there were other factors clawing at me that I had not realized. And the attitude of the Scottish Football Association – whom I had represented at three World Cups – was really infuriating me. It seemed to me that there was an ever-growing resentment about the success Rangers were enjoying as a club, and about me in particular.

For the first time since I had accepted the offer from David Holmes, I was having doubts. A whirlwind five years had gone by, with something happening every single day. Looking back, it must have been taking its toll on me. And the SFA's track record with me was playing a huge part in how I was feeling. It had started with the red card in my debut against Hibs – I was banned for three games and fined £5,000 – and escalated from there. Then there was a five-match ban for my red card in a game against Celtic in

August 1987. It was virtually incessant. I had a season ticket for the SFA offices at Park Gardens in Glasgow.

In February 1989 I was banned from the dugout for the rest of the season for arguing with the officials in a game against Dundee United. I think it might have been about them finding an extraordinary amount of time to add on, during which United equalized. My protests may have involved the heinous crime of me pointing at my watch.

In May 1990 they fined me a record £5,000 for a manager and extended a dugout ban by a further *two years* as a consequence of my having been spotted by STV cameras breaching the existing ban during a game against Hearts in February that year. It was ridiculous. The only report officially referring to the incident came from the SFA security adviser two months after the game, despite the fact that his original report – ten days after the fixture – did not refer to it in any way, shape or form. I am not denying I was in the tunnel, but the punishment didn't fit the crime. It was a trivial offence, but Rangers' response to the two-year ban called the punishment 'draconian'. And there was no right of appeal. Our club secretary, Campbell Ogilvie, argued that if the offence was worthy of a two-year ban and a £5,000 fine, why was it not mentioned in the first report? And are you telling me that other coaches and managers do not do this? But because they were not part of high-profile Rangers, they didn't have STV cameras snooping on them. There is little doubt that I was a target.

Then at the 1990–91 League Cup final – in which we beat Celtic 2–1 just eight days after the Aggie incident – I sprinted from the dugout to join in the celebrations with my players, and the clowns at the SFA decided that was a transgression of my ban! The game had finished, for heaven's sake. Were we to strip the sport of its emotion? How was I supposed to react to the fact that we had just beaten our biggest rivals in a cup final? It was utter madness.

It was my fourth League Cup triumph in five seasons – coincidentally, I won the same number in England as a player with Liverpool, before winning another as manager – so I had become pretty proficient in that competition. But the enjoyment levels were identical on both sides of the border. Mark Walters and the man I had recently appointed as captain to succeed Terry Butcher, Richard Gough, had scored to win in extra time. The atmosphere was through the roof. What did they expect me to do? Sit quietly and give thanks in prayer? Football is a highly emotional sport, and our officials did not seem to grasp that fact. They were banning feelings of joy, the very essence of our game.

Old Firm games have no match anywhere else on the planet. We were denied a treble that season by a Scottish Cup quarter-final defeat on 17 March – St Patrick's Day – at Parkhead in another crazy game. They had Peter Grant sent off, but then in an explosive spell we went down to eight men as Terry Hurlock, Mark Walters and Mark Hateley received red cards.

The men in blazers did not like Rangers and did not seem to get what football means to people, or how our fans felt when they went into work on a Monday after weekends like that. The tabloids and a television station had it in for me, so too the SFA, and the St Johnstone tea lady felt like the last straw.

Things started to unravel for me, but I was not the only one. Down south, things were becoming tough for my former teammate from club and country. My old chum Kenny Dalglish had resigned as manager of Liverpool on 22 February 1991, two days after a 4–4 draw against Everton in the FA Cup, a game in which his side lost the lead four times.

I can remember where and when I first heard about it. A bloke at security at Heathrow mentioned to me: 'I see your mate has resigned.'

'Which mate?' I asked, which will illustrate just how switched on to the situation I really was. That triggered the first approach from Anfield, and I had a phone call from the commercial manager there, Jim Kennifick, who was a dear friend and close to Peter Robinson, the chief executive. He posed the question and I answered it. I told him that I was not interested in succeeding Kenny.

I had a quality team at Ibrox and had done all the arduous work over the seasons since 1986. I felt that if we refreshed the line-up with the signing of a couple of key players every summer, we could go on winning titles for years. And this despite the departure of Terry Butcher. We were purring along in a football sense and put together a run of thirteen wins in fourteen games. At this point we were on our way to doing something Rangers had not achieved since 1935, namely winning three consecutive championships. And we'd have been going for five in a row had Terry not broken his leg in that game against Aberdeen in November 1987. Without that injury, I am convinced we would have gone on to win the championship that season too.

As it happens, there is not another club at that time I would even have considered leaving Glasgow Rangers for, and at no point did money come into the conversation. I did not tell anyone about the call from Jim Kennifick, and certainly not David Murray. Liverpool went quiet on the whole scene and Ronnie Moran took over from Kenny on a caretaker basis, a role he was in for ten games. Eventually I got a second call from Merseyside, and again I declined the offer.

However, my mind, with everything that was going on, began to drift. The authorities, the incident at McDiarmid Park, the press and the fact that my marriage had broken down were all getting to me. Plus, of course,

I had huge affection for Liverpool. Memories that were maybe clouding the issue.

And then came the breaking point. It was another fixture against St Johnstone at McDiarmid Park, a midweek game on a Tuesday night. It was 26 February 1991. I did not travel with the team but instead drove to Perth from Edinburgh with my mate Ian Blyth. I remember telling him that I felt something in the air that night.

We drew 1–1, and then after the game – and even though we were still clear at the top of the table – it actually all kicked off with Aggie Moffat . . . again! It was just astonishing that history could repeat itself. Same complaint, about mud on the dressing room floor, but this time she really went off on one and probably didn't realize where my head was. She told me that she was so angry she was going to see the St Johnstone chairman about me. There were reports of crockery being thrown but I'm not so sure about that. Perhaps the naughty tabloids suggested it happened, to justify their 'Storm in a Teacup' headlines? Anyway, off she stormed out of the dressing room, except she did not realize that I was right behind her, all the way to the boardroom.

Geoff Brown was their club chairman at the time, and as she told her story to him I was looking over her shoulder and listening to her rant. And then I gave him my version. I remember that he put his arm on me, and I asked him to take it away. At that point, I knew I was close to losing it totally.

On the way back to Edinburgh with Ian, I told him the story and admitted I had embarrassed myself. But I knew something had snapped. The next morning, I rang Peter Robinson at Liverpool and asked him if the offer of the job was still on the table. I told him that if it was, I would come and talk. It was and I did.

At the time, I believed I needed out of Scotland and away from the mentality in the game there that doesn't like success. Please let me underline that this was never about money. If it was, the chairman would have thrashed that out. There is an old tactic that managers use when they want a wage rise, which is to persuade a friendly football writer to publish a story about such-and-such a club being interested in said manager, so that his current club will enhance his deal to get him to stay. A fantasy, but one that works to hook your current employers.

There was no need for that nonsense with David Murray. If ever I had employed that tactic, he would have seen right through it, but it would never have happened because of the relationship we had. In any case, I met David Moores, the major shareholder at Anfield, at his home in Ormskirk. He offered me the job, and I asked for twenty-four hours to consider.

I slept on it and woke up knowing that my time at Rangers was coming to an end.

What I had agreed was that I would stay at Ibrox until the end of the season and leave with – hopefully – another championship in the bag. There were still – by the time the story came out – four league games to play. I wanted my third title in a row, the fourth of my Rangers career. It would have been the perfect scenario to announce it then. Or so I reckoned.

But that is not how it worked out.

To this day, I have no idea how David Murray found out, but one night we were together in a restaurant for supper before we then both went home. But within ten minutes of me getting back, he called me at my flat and asked if he could come and see me.

It was a lovely spring evening, and we sat down on the wall outside my block of flats, and he said: 'You're going to Liverpool, aren't you?'

No niceties. He had just sensed something. No one could have told him anything. It was as if he was psychic. It was the strength of our relationship and the closeness that had built up over the years that meant he knew me so well. He felt something was not right. And also there was a lot of press speculation about me returning to Liverpool. So, I told him the truth, and he immediately told me I was making the biggest mistake of my life. He suggested

I take a year or two off and just become an observer on the board helping run football matters while Walter Smith got on with it in the dressing room. He even suggested that I just go and travel for a while.

In retrospect, it was great advice from David, but I was not particularly good at taking that from anyone. Maybe later in life it would have worked, but at the age of thirty-seven I could not see me sitting quietly in the directors' box, or resisting the temptation to sprint down to the technical area to Walter, or have a rant in the dressing room. It just was not in my personality to sit quietly.

The truth is that I eventually asked Walter to come with me to Anfield, and at first he agreed. I remember I was sitting in a sauna with him and Phil Boersma at a hotel near Ibrox one afternoon and broke the news to them that I had been offered the Liverpool job. I told them that I was leaving and that I wanted them both to come with me. Phil, a Scouser and ex-Liverpool player, was of course all for it. He was going home, and initially Walter said he would join us. But overnight he changed his mind and said he could not leave Rangers. He wanted to stay and take his chances. And, to be fair, things worked out and he went on to make history at the club he loved.

I hadn't had a proper holiday in five years. I had been abroad, but every day was spent on the phone dealing with Rangers' business, players and transfer targets. I had been totally immersed in the affairs of the club. I wasn't particularly good at listening to the chairman's advice in my situation, even though I wasn't shy about handing out mine. Years later, in 2001, I did quiz Alex Ferguson as to why he was quitting Manchester United – although he did change his mind that time – and walking out on a phenomenally successful club. But, of course, here was me doing exactly that.

Jobs don't become available very often at winning clubs – recently, Liverpool appointing Arne Slot to take over from Jürgen Klopp is a rare example. Positions normally only come up at places that are toiling. I did not do my due diligence at Anfield. It was not the Liverpool I had left. The club and indeed the city were still struggling to get over the Hillsborough disaster. Understandably, it had affected everyone very deeply.

I didn't consider David's advice, but I should have. And he did not appreciate my plan to stay until the end of the season either. My belief was that, just as we had with the Mo Johnston signing, we could have kept it all under wraps, thereby causing as little upheaval as possible, but it was all taken out of my hands, and David insisted I leave at once.

And so, on 16 April 1991, I faced the media and David Murray announced my departure. It was rare although not unique for a departing manager to have a press conference – I think Kenny Dalglish did it at

Liverpool – but I owed them that. It was brief, I remember that, and David said I had to go at once because 'No man is bigger than Rangers football club', and that was why it had to be done immediately.

But I made a point of saying: 'I would like to state that I wanted to stay until the end of the season but it has been decided by the board that it's in the best interests of the football club if I go now and I have to accept that.' I added: 'I feel as if I've gone as far as I will be *allowed* to go and try and achieve success at this football club.'

Looking back, I still think that forcing me to leave early was the wrong decision because of the upheaval it caused in the last handful of games.

When I left Ibrox, Rangers were two points clear of Aberdeen – in the days of two points for a win – with four matches to go. They beat St Mirren and Dundee United with 1–0 scorelines, before losing 3–0 to Motherwell, thereby setting up a nerve-wracking climax.

It had been a nervous win at Love Street on 20 April, with a rare goal from Sandy Robertson, and the team had key players missing, but Richard Gough and Mo Johnston were back for the United game, won by a goal from Ian Ferguson. Then came the crushing defeat by Motherwell at Fir Park, in which Davie Cooper played his part for the opposition, and which saw Archie Knox in the technical area for the first time as Walter's assistant.

So, going into the last game against Aberdeen at Ibrox, Rangers' opponents were top on the old goal average system, which meant Walter had to win. I do remember calling him and wishing him all the best for that spring day. It was 11 May and I was in charge of Liverpool as we hosted Spurs in our final match of the season, a 2–0 victory that ensured us second place in the old First Division. That was my priority, but I was delighted to hear that two Mark Hateley goals – the player I had hunted down for years – had won Walter and the lads the championship; the third instalment of what went on to become nine in a row.

Anyway, after the presser in the Blue Room off I popped, heading for Merseyside. Meanwhile, the chairman did not mess about, and within three days he was back in the Blue Room unveiling my assistant Walter as my successor.

I should not have left. Years later, I remember telling Philippe Clement – whom I helped appoint as manager at Ibrox – being manager of Rangers would be either the best or worst job he would ever have. And he grew to understand that. He was in tears when he was sacked. He eventually got it about the support, the history and passion. Clement, who had gone to Norwich City and proven his talent, had to go because of his failure to win the title, but that wasn't an issue with me, and I should not have gone.

Everything that season seemed to be about emotion; it

was very curious. In Europe, we had beaten Valletta of Malta 10–0 on aggregate and in the second leg I let our goalkeeper, Chris Woods, take a penalty . . . which he missed. I do not know why I allowed that to happen. It shows a huge amount of disrespect for the opposition and, all these years later, I apologize to our opponents. Goalies should not be near spot kicks. Unless they are trying to save them.

In any case, we were knocked out in the next round by a fabulous team in Red Star Belgrade, who featured Darko Pančev and the highly talented Robert Prosinečki, who went on to play for Real Madrid and Barcelona. It was all over in the first leg when we lost 3–0 in Belgrade, although we recovered a bit of dignity in a 1–1 draw at Ibrox in the second leg.

On top of all that, on 5 April 1991 Ian Durrant made his comeback 916 days after the horror tackle by Neil Simpson at Pittodrie. It was to be my last game in charge of the club. Fate was playing its cards all over the place.

Looking back, the situation triggered a tsunami of emotion over the next weeks. I remember leaving Ibrox and driving south towards Liverpool with Phil Boersma. We stopped for a coffee and fuel at Killington Lake Services on the M6 and I had a moment of doubt. I asked him if we were doing the right thing. Phil, naturally, was excited about going back to the club he loved, but he looked at me and said: 'It's your call.' I looked away for a moment and then we got back in the car and continued to drive south.

It is hard to recall what was running through my mind. I was, of course, wrapped up in my new job, and there was plenty of work to be done. But, in my head, I could not help reflecting on five astonishing years of my life and how it had come to this. Maybe I should have taken David Murray's advice and sat on the board for a year or two. I was already a director after all. Was I being too hasty saying yes to my old club on Merseyside?

I am extremely proud of my five years at our iconic football club. The fans flocked back in my first season as we trekked back from the wilderness and soon we pushed the average gate up to over 20,000. The second term it was 30,000-plus, and then the next one again it was pushing 40,000. We did the right thing. On and off the park.

I had managed Glasgow Rangers for 257 games – playing in seventy-three of them – and had won 125 of 193 league fixtures. Look, I know I went to the right club at the right time and the stars aligned for me. The funds were there for us to buy the big-name players, but I'd argue that it was my profile and familiarity with them that persuaded them to come to Scotland. Their mantra was: 'If it is good enough for Souness then let's give it a try.' We got them in the door and I give thanks every day that we did. It was a five-star five years.

13

Glasgow Strangers

And so the afterlife began. Phil and I drained our coffee cups and continued south on the M6 for the next instalment of my great footballing adventure.

I have tried to live my life without looking over my shoulder, rather stretching out towards the next challenge – something that is best illustrated by the fact that I am currently living in my twenty-seventh house! Maybe that is one little bit of sadness, that I have never been able to settle anywhere. Should I have stayed much longer-term at Rangers? I do not really know. David Murray did tell me I would regret the decision to leave and, looking back, he was probably right. I have had the most incredible life and mostly it has been a breeze for me, although maybe once or twice I bit off more than I could chew.

Still, Rangers were behind me, and I have never been one to be looking in the rear-view mirror for too long.

On arrival at Liverpool, I initially had a period staying in a hotel, and then I bought a delightful home in Knutsford in Cheshire and moved in. Life was grand.

I would train with the players in the morning, matching everything they were doing except playing on a Saturday afternoon. I'd then have an hour in the office clearing my desk with the help of my fabulous secretary Sheila Walsh, and then I would go back into the gym for an hour before heading home, where I'd go to bed for an hour, just to have a nap.

In the evening, I would go over to Mere Golf Resort & Spa for another session in the gym, and then on somewhere for dinner. In retrospect, I had a problem for a couple of years after giving up playing, in the sense that I was addicted to going to the gym. Otherwise, I was living the life of an incredibly lucky 38-year-old.

But I had an unknown problem. I looked and felt fit, and my tolerance for extreme exercise was very good. However, I wasn't sleeping properly. I would wake up in the middle of the night, tired with a bursting headache, and take two Solpadeine, then lie awake for hours thinking about the job. My lifestyle as a single man, as well as my love of eating and drinking late, would not have been conducive to a good night's sleep. As I have mentioned, there is a history of heart problems in my family. So, with this in mind, I asked the team doctor at Anfield to make an appointment for an ECG – an electrocardiogram – to check the rate and rhythm of my heart. I was so tired I embarrassingly fell asleep during the procedure. That was how bad it had become.

After the ECG, the consultant, Derek Rowlands, said he'd seen nothing too concerning but he suggested to me that I might want to undergo another ECG, this time on a treadmill. This was for a test used to diagnose heart conditions in which they increase the speed and incline of the treadmill at three-minute intervals. The medical term for it is the Bruce Protocol, named after its inventor who, interestingly enough for all Scots, was Robert Bruce! I coped admirably. I got to eighteen minutes, and they said that anyone who could get this far could not have too much wrong with them. But then they admitted that it did show some irregularities.

After telling me the results, Derek Rowlands offered me two options. He said I could either come back in a year, or have an angiogram, the definitive test that reveals any blocking or narrowing of the arteries. That procedure involves injecting a dye through an artery in your wrist or groin, which they then scan to see how your coronary arteries are performing.

And at the time all this was going on, something happened that would change my life for ever. I had been separated from my first wife for three years and I was living the life of a single man, but one night I met a young woman who was to become my wife.

It was destiny. Incredibly, both Mike Summerbee, once of Manchester City, *and* a friend in Scotland had independently tried to organize a blind date between me and a woman called Karen Levy. Someone somewhere was trying to tell us something. I remember at the time, on the front page of *Cheshire Life* – a local magazine – there was a picture of a group of people coming back from a champagne-tasting trip to France . . . and one of them was Karen. And I thought to myself: 'She's an attractive woman . . .'

One night, in a wine bar, Karen was with a friend, and I was with pals Johnny Dexter and Gerry Ritchie and journalist Des Kelly. I said to Johnny: 'They are attractive girls, why don't you ask them if they want to join us for a glass of champagne?' Karen said, 'No.' I said to Johnny: 'OK, go back and ask them if they would like a *bottle* of champagne?' She said, 'No,' again.

After two knock-backs, we just sent over a bottle of very nice champagne called Dom Pérignon. Then we invited ourselves to join them and ended up having a fabulous evening.

At the end of the night, I said to her, 'Let me give you my number,' but she wouldn't take it and instead offered to give me hers. We didn't see one another for at least seven days or so because of my busy schedule, but did have phone calls that went on in to the early hours of the morning. I was getting the feeling that this was someone incredibly special; the lengthy calling was something I had never done before. So, we arranged a date.

I had her address and directions to her house. I also had a single rose on the passenger seat of my car and two dozen in the boot. The reason for this was that I was 99 per cent sure that she was as gorgeous as I remembered. But there was 1 per cent of nagging doubt, a confusion caused by the fact that on the night we met I'd had way over my normal intake of champagne.

I struggled to find the street she was living in, so I called her mobile phone and she guided me to her house. As I got to the end of her cul-de-sac, my attention was drawn to a house on the left-hand side where there was a blond-haired individual on the phone in the bay window. I assumed this was the person I was talking to on the phone. As I got closer, I was horrified to see it was a guy. I thought: 'I must have been properly pissed the other night . . . I've got a date with a man.' I nearly slammed the car into reverse. I was looking at the single red rose, and it was looking at me, and I was thinking: 'Get yourself out of this one, Graeme.'

But just as I was hatching my escape plan, I saw someone on the right side of another house waving at me.

It was Karen. I had been looking at the wrong house. She got the twenty-four roses. *And* the single one. The blond guy in the bay window was Karen's friend Mark Galazka. I became very friendly with him and his wife Sue.

However, within a couple of weeks our relationship had become very intense, and I knew this was the real thing. On our third date I began wondering how I was going to tell Karen about the serious surgery I was about to undergo. I was dressed in my latest Versace gear, thinking I looked extremely smart, and I blurted out the words, 'I'm going in for open-heart surgery in four days,' which made her take a deep breath and sit back in her seat. She has since confirmed that she thought she was having dinner with a madman that night.

My cardiologist, Derek Rowlands, had told me that three arteries were severely blocked and that, while I could leave it, this might be dangerous because of my family history and my line of work. The surgeon would be a wonderful Norwegian called Geir Grøtte, who informed me that while he was happy to be operating on me, he would much prefer to be working on a real sportsman like a Norwegian cross-country skier.

We drew 1–1 with Portsmouth in the FA Cup semi-final at Highbury on Sunday, 5 April 1992, and Geir told me he would do the operation two days later, on the Tuesday. So, on the Monday evening, I was in hospital preparing for my operation at 7 a.m. the following day when a nurse came in and told me she had to shave me totally from the armpits down. And when she finished, she said: 'Right, now stand on that chair.' She then started to mark the veins on the inside of my legs with a felt-tip pen in case they were needed for the procedure. For me, this was the reality check. When what was happening became real.

An hour after the shaving, just as I was accepting my lot, surgeon Geir came into my room to explain the procedure for the following day. Given this was now after 9 p.m., I suggested that he would be going home to have an early bed to prepare for my operation in the morning. 'Oh no,' he smiled, 'I'm off to the pub!' He said there was this bar near the hospital that served an incredibly special real ale he loved, and he promised me he would only have two pints. Man of his word, I think. Given that I am still here thirty-four years later, he obviously did a good job.

I was supposed to be in the hospital for ten days but I actually ended up being there for twenty-eight because I picked up an infection. While I was confined to my bed, Liverpool drew the Portsmouth replay 0–0 at Villa Park, getting through to Wembley after extra time and penalties, but I had bigger concerns.

I was now back in intensive care for the second time in ten days and there was a clock on the wall that I gazed at all night. It was the one and only time in my life I felt scared. I remember looking at it and telling myself not to go to sleep because this was how you died. I was thirty-eight years old.

But even then, Rangers came back into my life. Walter Smith and David Murray both came to see me as I was recovering. The day Walter visited me, he said: 'You won't like this, but I have something I have to tell you.'

When I left, Archie Knox had quit as Alex Ferguson's assistant at Manchester United to join Rangers as number two to Walter. He was friendly with Brian Kidd, who had taken on Archie's role at Old Trafford. Brian called Archie to get him to pass something on to Walter, who was in turn to tell me. Phil Thompson – my former teammate, who was now on the coaching staff at Anfield – had bad-mouthed me in the Liverpool boot room after a game with United.

While I had been in hospital, Manchester United had lost 2–0 at Anfield, ending their chances of winning the league that year. Ian Rush and my former Rangers player Mark Walters, who had taken the same road south as me, had scored. And in front of Alex Ferguson and others from United – our biggest rivals – Phil said that the changes we were making were all wrong. And he was critical of some of the players I had signed.

Phil should not have expressed his opinions in front of any opposition, never mind, of all people, the coaching staff of Manchester United. One of the first things I did when I left hospital was to confront him and explain to him face-to-face why I was sacking him.

And, unfortunately, it was not the end of my heart issues. Because of my cholesterol situation, I have subsequently had five stents inserted, which sure beats getting your sternum cracked open. To all the medics who have looked after me these thirty-four years: a huge thank you. And a special one to the cardiologist who looks after me today, Suneel Talwar, who has an Indian father and a Scottish mother. He looks after me like I am a member of his family.

I repeat: I have been a lucky man, on and off the park.

So, at that time – apart from calls to and from Walter and David – Rangers were not all that much in my thoughts. Staying alive was the big priority. But over the following years there were moments of re-engagement. A few years ago, when things were not going well at Rangers, directors Dave King and Paul Murray approached me to come back in some capacity. I had lunch with them in Scott's restaurant in Mayfair in London, but it was never clear exactly what they wanted from me and I could not see how I could help them. I felt that me being involved would alleviate the pressure on them for a few weeks; but, long-term, nothing was going to change. So I declined.

And then I was part of the interview process looking for a manager to succeed Michael Beale in 2023. I thought that Philippe Clement interviewed best of all, but I took a real shine to Frank Lampard. Frank had the most wonderful career as a player and had had several managerial jobs by then. He comes from a footballing family – I played against his father Frank many times – and apart from being a fabulous player, he was also successful in his business outside the game.

So here was a young man wanting to be the manager of Glasgow Rangers in the hothouse (and sometimes madhouse) of the west of Scotland. I can remember my second and third questions to him during the interview, the second one being about his relationship with Chelsea and whether he could get loan players out of there. I also asked him, 'Is your relationship with Manchester City still strong enough to get players from them?' He said yes to both queries. Given Rangers' financial restrictions at the time, I thought that was an obvious route we should have been exploiting.

I was very much taken by his passion and by his desire to return to the front line as a manager, something that would put his reputation to the test. But he also would not have been going to Glasgow Rangers completely blind. His wife Christine – who is from Northern Ireland – comes from a Rangers-supporting family. I try to tell anybody who I know is going to work for Rangers about the enormity of the football club, the thing that I'd had to find out forty years ago. What you must understand is that, while the support for you to do well is massive, you also must be prepared for when things are not going so well.

Had Rangers and Celtic got to join the English Premier League (although I feel that ship has now sailed), then they would ultimately have been challenging for the title. Both Rangers and Celtic could build 100,000-seater stadiums and there would be a lock-out every home game.

My life has been one crazy, exciting, outrageous rollercoaster ride, but my time at Glasgow Rangers was just off the charts, in terms of everything that happened in and around that wonderful football club. We changed things that needed changing, and I am proud of that. Rangers were as big as any club in the United Kingdom at the time, but television money has changed everything now. Given the increasing focus on English football, the Scottish League is way in the wake of what is happening even in the Championship. The financial gulf is massive. Winning the title in Scotland is worth around £5 million in prize money. Clubs in the second tier in England are getting that *each* from Sky.

People in days still to come, long after this generation has moved on, can judge my legacy at the club.

I am not here to second-guess what they will think. The stars aligned for me. It was the right job at the right time because of a combination of circumstances that will never come together again. At that age, I was aggressive, fearless and was presented with a unique opportunity, given what had happened at Heysel and the consequences of the Lord Justice Taylor report about all-seated stadiums. Here was a massive football club that had lost its way and needed shaking awake into the time in which it was living. I feel we accomplished that.

Before 1986, there had been a small-minded mentality at the club, but we changed all that and signed the captain of England and several of his teammates. We became the equal of any club in the United Kingdom.

When I arrived, Ally McCoist was on about £300 a week, and I remember summoning him and Ian Durrant up to my office at the top of the marble staircase and telling them to sit down.

I think they have subsequently said they thought they were getting fined or transfer-listed, but I pulled out their wage slips and asked them if this was all they were getting paid. They nodded and I started laughing. I instantly more than doubled their salaries. If the demands are high, the rewards should be too, and I would say they stepped up because of that show of faith. It was important to follow the lead shown by David Holmes in his dealings with Dundee United over Walter Smith and pay the going rate.

We were all involved in the rebuilding of Rangers as a united force.

It was achieved because we created something special; there was a real sense of togetherness about the place. Everyone was pulling in the same direction. How different it was when I went to Liverpool. I was confronted almost immediately by three players – Steve McMahon, Peter Beardsley and Ray Houghton – who all wanted to leave. That is the same Ray Houghton who could have been the first high-profile Catholic signing at Rangers. I told them to get the clubs who were interested to contact me at once. I should not have done that. I should have told them they would have to be patient and wait until I could find replacements for them. That was a situation I was not used to – players wanting to quit. And you will recall that I seldom took the easy option.

In my time at Ibrox only Davie Cooper asked to get away and that was because I could not guarantee him a starting place. I regret the fallouts I had with the likes of Graham Roberts and Terry Butcher, and I should have been the bigger man and met them halfway. That was my lack of experience back then. Looking back, what I would say is that I was much too tough as a manager and that was down to my education as a player at Anfield, where I witnessed the ways of Joe Fagan and Ronnie Moran.

Another thing about my time in Glasgow was that I should have been cuter about the situation that evolved when I was playing. I was making challenges on players who would roll over as if their leg was broken, trying to get me a yellow card – or even better, a red. There is no doubt that the opposition – particularly Celtic and Aberdeen – would instruct their players to go down and make the most of any challenge I had made. Unfortunately, that was the precursor to what has become normal in our game now. It is simulation. But I can honestly say I have never once tried to get someone in trouble by going down too easily in my whole career. The vast majority of people I played against – and remember I played in Italy for two years and all over Europe with Liverpool – were not as bad as what I was confronted with when I went to Glasgow. Of course, I was caught by a challenge once or twice, but I did not want people to know when I had been hurt. Call me naive or honest.

You cannot let the atmosphere get to you when you play for Rangers and, trust me, it could be hostile in some matches. Old Firm games and their high tempo and levels of excitement, for example, were mostly unmatched by anything I have played in – and don't forget, I performed in three European Cup finals. Not to put too fine a point on it, but Glasgow – as its citizens often reflect – can be mental at times. Although I have to say the best atmosphere I ever faced was the European tie against Dynamo Kyiv when we won 2–0 at Ibrox. The stadium was volcanic that night.

What a time it was back then in the late eighties. I was manager of Rangers before Alex Ferguson was at Manchester United, before the Channel Tunnel was started, when Margaret Thatcher was prime minister, Timothy Dalton was James Bond and before Andy Murray was born. And beer was about eighty pence a pint. Time marches on.

Even relationships with the press were on a different planet from the bland, club-media-department-controlled environment of today. I argued with reporters in a way I know does not happen now – in press conferences they would work in pairs trying to trip me up. If I answered a question that did not take them where they wanted, then the other half of the tag team would push it in a different direction. But eventually I did work it out and managed to avoid most of the traps. I left Glasgow Rangers without my detractors laying a finger on me and with my dignity intact, despite the efforts of some.

I think back now and smile. And that, of course, is the best way to remember anything.

Half a decade with Rangers is such a small percentage of my ever-increasing lifespan, but its impact on me has been way out of proportion. It was an incredibly special time at a very special club trying to make a special support happy.

What a life I have lived, from attending the same Edinburgh school as the great Dave Mackay, following in his footsteps to Tottenham Hotspur and then onwards on my own journey. How many schools have produced two Scotland captains?

You have no option but to embrace change, but sometimes I listen and watch people talking about football and think: 'I know more than you.' I won twenty-five trophies with Middlesbrough, Liverpool, Sampdoria, Rangers, Blackburn and Galatasaray. A Spurs fan pointed out to me recently that I have won more as an individual than my first club have in their entire history. I must have played in some good teams.

It has been some adventure.

When I was unveiled at the press conference at Ibrox I said:

> It was my ambition one day to become a manager, but I did not expect a big job so soon.
>
> I won't have any regrets about leaving Italy because my life is that of a professional footballer and this is a step up the ladder. I am new to management and

> obviously I will make mistakes, but I hope they will not be big ones.
>
> I would not have taken this job if I thought it was not right for me. Rangers are one of the biggest clubs in British football.
>
> I have no reservations whatsoever.

I think I should let you in on a secret. When I was a boy, me being the youngest of three sons, my mother would point to me and say to my father on a regular basis: 'There's something definitely wrong with that one, because wherever he goes, there is never a dull moment.'

At the tender age of seventy-three, I haven't let Mum down yet.

Afterword: And Then What?

By Chick Young

In all my decades observing our great game, I have never witnessed anything that came close to the Souness years at Ibrox. Two years or so after he left, he came back to Glasgow with Karen and asked me to pick him up at the airport, which I did. On the way towards the city, he asked me if I could divert from the motorway to show Ibrox Stadium to his wife. She had never previously set eyes on the place. Karen was in the front passenger seat, Graeme in the back.

In those days you could turn off Edmiston Drive and circumnavigate the ground anticlockwise from the Copland Road end, where Walter Smith's statue now stands. Graeme was clearly still in awe of the place and was telling Karen that very fact. And then he fell silent as we drove slowly round.

Only then did he speak, and not really to us, but more

as a reflection of what he really felt. And just under his breath, he uttered: 'I should never have left . . .'

He came. He saw. He conquered. And then he pissed off.

As Graeme and Phil Boersma disappeared over the horizon and down the M6 to Merseyside, behind them Clydeside and beyond was collectively wondering what on earth had just happened. Five years. World wars have lasted longer. Vacuum cleaners come with lifetime guarantee promises. Meanwhile, Souness and Rangers indulged in what, in retrospect, was a brief and fiery affair.

But it is a love that clearly endures because generations of Rangers supporters are still awed by what he achieved in those incredible years. Just five bloody years. The blooded ones were to come after the turn of the century.

As a football journalist in the late eighties I was scared to sleep, petrified that I might miss the next instalment of the greatest soap opera that ever was in the Scottish national game. Those of us in the business wondered if life could ever possibly be the same again. Surprise, excitement, disbelief, shock, awe, horror. There was a cocktail of emotions served daily.

When Souness and Rangers split it was a divorce of Taylor and Burton proportions. The football world drooled for gossip. Walter Smith – the apprentice who had learned Souness's sorcery – was asked to step up, with

David Murray insisting there was never another option. Walter raised his hands in celebration that spring afternoon in 1991 against Aberdeen at Ibrox when Mark Hateley's goals dismantled the Dons, but Graeme was entitled to take at least one ear of the silverware.

Walter later admitted in his autobiography, *Mr Smith*:

> Technically the first trophy I won was the title in 1991 – but it's not a victory campaign I can take much credit for.
>
> Mind you, I was fairly clear in my own mind that day that if the game was lost – and the championship with it – then I would carry the can. I was also conscious that if we won the championship much of the credit would go to Graeme for putting us in the right position. It was Catch-22.

Make up your own mind. Souness was in charge for thirty-two of the season's thirty-six games and Walter for four. They won twenty-four of them, drew seven and lost five. So, what Walter said was probably kind of true, I think. But while Smith went on to carve his name in the club's history he knew there could be no nine in a row without the foundations of the three laid down by his mate. It could have been four bar Terry Butcher's injury, the one that Souness believes cost them the 1987–88 championship and hiccupped the sequence. Nine was the Holy Grail because Celtic had achieved it under Jock Stein between 1966 and 1974. Consequently, their old rivals hungered for it. Lusted for it. And Souness and Smith – collectively and then individually – made it happen. Smith inherited a team that was purring.

Graeme, meanwhile, on his own admission, failed to do his due diligence on a Liverpool side that was beginning to wheeze. It would be a little severe to suggest that they needed a carer, not a manager, but too many had already been at the top of the hill. Walter, in the end, became a wise old fox, but he never forgot what he learned from his younger friend. The bond remained tight until his dying day.

Managers of Rangers have come and gone in these succeeding decades . . . some of them having to sneak out the back door. From day one there had been a trickle of eight – although Jock Wallace was given the job twice – by the time Souness was appointed. That was before the flood. In fact, it was a waterfall of Niagaran proportions. I'm surprised Noah never got a call. Walter Smith, Dick Advocaat, Alex McLeish, Paul Le Guen, Walter again, Ally McCoist, Mark Warburton, Pedro Caixinha, Stevie Gerrard, Giovanni van Bronckhorst, Michael Beale, Philippe Clement, Russell Martin, Danny Röhl, Derek McInnes.

There were fourteen permanent appointments between

1991 and 2025. And during that time Rangers became a little unsteady on their feet. In fact, they fell prostrate. It was complicated, but basically Rangers FC entered administration in February 2012 – Saint Valentine's Day – over debt to HMRC. Not quite the massacre, but that was in the post. The club went into liquidation nine months later.

I recall a briefing for the broadcast media only, at which there were to be no recording devices – by this time I had sold my soul to the BBC – and I asked then-chairman Alastair Johnston if the club could go bust. He said nothing but simply nodded. It became known as 'Nod-gate'.

It was maybe the only time in its history that the football club matched the Souness era's ability to monopolize airtime and headline space. There were plots and subplots. And subplots of subplots. And . . . well, you get the hang of it.

I do remember the then-chief executive, Martin Bain, claiming to me that the debt had been reduced from around £32 million to around £18 million, which, he argued, for an operation the size of Rangers was a highly manageable sum. A small mortgage on a palatial home, if you will. Turned out it wasn't quite that simple.

The club was deducted ten points in 2011–12 and was consequently relegated to the Third Division – the fourth tier of the senior game – from where it had to claw its way up the mountain under the stewardship of Ally McCoist.

It all meant that Sir David Murray's time had come to a

sticky end, although he has always denied any wrongdoing. He gave up the chairmanship in 2002, returning to the position two years later. He sold the club to Craig Whyte in May 2011 for £1 and the inheritance of the debt, subject to various other demands, and the meltdown continued. It was a sad ending for a man who had formed such a bond with Graeme and with whom that friendship endures.

Whyte meanwhile proved to be as useful as a chocolate fireguard. It was Murray who made possible the fantasy signings of the mid-nineties, but Gascoigne and the rest of the big-name stars were only following a trail blazed by Butcher and Woods and Roberts and Wilkins.

By 2016 Rangers were back in the top division, and by 2021 had won the title again under Stevie Gerrard – just in time to stop Celtic, who had hoovered up championships while Rangers were absent from the top league, winning an unprecedented ten in a row.

Of course this had little to do with the Magnificent Bastard. Although, on his own admission, he was never one to take the easy option. He was off to coach Liverpool, Galatasaray, Southampton, Torino, Benfica, Blackburn Rovers and Newcastle United.

And always a man to court a headline, Graeme inspired an iconic image in 1996 when he planted a huge Galatasaray flag on the centre spot of the pitch of bitter rivals Fenerbahçe after a Turkish Cup final between the clubs. It was all to do with disrespectful comments from a Fenerbahçe director, who called Graeme 'a cripple' in reference to his heart surgery. Graeme spotted the aforementioned director during the celebrations and thought, 'I'll show you who is a cripple,' and planted the flag.

The opposing fans didn't see the funny side and were determined to discuss the matter at closer quarters, but Graeme said he found a bit of pace and made it to the sanctuary of the tunnel. If you're wondering how that was all viewed in Istanbul, think of him planting a Rangers flag into the centre spot at Celtic Park.

You can say what you want about the man, but you cannot deny that he is box-office.

Forty years after his departure, there is undying warmth and affection for Souness from the Rangers legions. I have walked across Edmiston Drive outside the stadium main entrance with him and the adoration is palpable. And the parting is Red Sea-esque. Except with selfies.

You can sense the respect and gratitude in the air when he revisits the stadium, not just from the support but from the players who served him. Mark Hateley, Ian Durrant, John Brown, Richard Gough, even Ally McCoist, all still call him 'gaffer'. I have watched them in his company and he remains king among even that level of Rangers royalty. McCoist – who occasionally appears on radio and television in the same low-profile way as, say, Donald Trump – is cheeky to him, but is clearly still in awe. 'I wish I had a pound for every time he was going to kill me,' he said.

> We played a game at Parkhead and Celtic beat us 2–0. Graeme was still playing at the time and he came into the dressing room and I can see he is still raging. He turned to me and got his finger right in my face and said I was a disgrace. He added that I was the worst player on the park. I could see Ian Durrant urging me to shut up and take it but I couldn't stop myself. I was shaking my head. He shouted at me about shaking my head. And then I said I wasn't the worst player. He was. I swear to God, his face went scarlet and I thought he was going to kill me.
>
> But I do love him. He is the best pundit in the game. We are great pals now. No one will forget what he did for the club. He has a remarkable presence and working with him was an education. He only wanted us to be winners. Graeme took my game to another level and he came to Rangers at a time when we had lost our way and needed help. He sorted that. He should be very proud of everything he achieved.

And Walter was never in doubt. He wrote in *Mr Smith*:

> In all that time I cannot recall one falling out between us. It was a partnership I look back on with affection

> because I gained a lot from it. There were a lot of times when we found ourselves under scrutiny by the media. Times when the decisions which were taken were not popular with the support. Or with the players. Or, very often, with the football authorities. And universally unpopular with fans of every other club in the country. That was never something which worried Graeme. And, gradually, it was not something which worried me either.
>
> We were different personalities but on major issues we were in agreement.

He added: 'My times with him were unforgettable. Frantic. Furious. Fiery. The stormiest period of my football life and yet I was sad when it came to an end and Graeme left for Liverpool – even though I was handed the manager's job.'

Walter Smith took Graeme's baton and ran with it. The spend, spend, spend days of the mid-eighties were eclipsed by those of the mid-nineties and, as Walter went on to gather twenty-one major trophies, he shelled out a fortune along the way. Trevor Steven, Duncan Ferguson, Basile Boli, Brian Laudrup, Jörg Albertz, Lorenzo Amoruso, Pedro Mendes, Nikica Jelavić . . . oh, and Paul Gascoigne. Among others.

Gazza, nutty as a fruitcake but a diamond of a man,

was another in the headline-making hall of fame. And he too fell in love with Rangers. I can only imagine Souness managing Gascoigne. And what a midfield combination that would have been if time machines were readily available.

Dick Advocaat and Alex McLeish hardly applied the financial brakes either. Giovanni van Bronckhorst, Arthur Numan, Andrei Kanchelskis, Michael Mols, Tore Andre Flo, Stefan Klos, Ronald de Boer and Tugay all came to sign for the Dutchman. Big Eck brought in Mikel Arteta, Shota Arveladze and Dado Pršo among others, but spending was being trimmed a little by then.

In 1993, under Walter, there was that complicated and controversial Champions League set-up where Rangers and Marseille played for Group A supremacy. It would all go to the last game for a place in the inaugural Champions League final. The last eight clubs were split into two groups of four, with the top two teams qualifying for the final. Going into the last game, Rangers were level on points with the French club.

Marseille went on to beat AC Milan 1–0, but it emerged that they had fixed a French league match six days before that game, thus allowing them to focus on the final. They were stripped of the French championship and relegated. And then they were banned from the following season's Champions League . . . but not stripped of their win that season. All very curious. There were huge suspicions of subterfuge at the time.

Walter also had to contend with the four-foreigner rule being introduced in 1991–92, a plan aimed at the encouragement of native talent. The highly popular BBC television comedy *Only an Excuse?*, which liked a dig at Scottish players, stingingly referred to it as the 'seven diddies rule'.

Meanwhile, the heroes of Graeme's story of the astonishing eighties will have their own tales to tell.

David Holmes is a spritely 91-year-old now, who at one point – in 1990 – went back to Falkirk, his first football love. He was also in charge of Dundee for a while. He remains warmly welcomed at Ibrox.

Mo Johnston's name still triggers debate wherever Scottish football is discussed and he is still nursing that impish sense of humour. After Rangers, he went to Everton before coming back to Scotland with Hearts and then Falkirk. He moved to America in 1996 and played in Kansas. He was later in Canada and Florida. He scored fourteen goals in thirty-eight international appearances and did eventually settle in the States, where he still lives.

There was no more famous transfer in Scottish football than that of Mo. And his agent, Bill McMurdo, is still at the forefront of negotiations. Among his clients back in the day was Derek Ferguson, and now Bill operates on behalf of Derek's boy Lewis, who plays in Serie A with Bologna. Another of his players was Frank McAvennie and that was the route to goal when Graeme fancied Macca as the first high-profile Catholic signing. To this day, McMurdo insists it was a non-starter. And McAvennie has seconded that emotion to me.

Chris Woods – former England goalkeeper – had a meandering career after leaving Ibrox and went to Sheffield Wednesday, Reading, Colorado, Southampton and Burnley. But he couldn't stay away from Glasgow. He is currently the goalkeeping coach with the Scotland team and travelled as part of the squad to the 2026 World Cup.

There was actually a picture in Graeme's time of the English players posing in kilts, with 'Mac' added to their surnames, as in 'MacWoods'. One of the players was of course Terry Butcher, who was only behind Mo Johnston in terms of products from the factory of headline-makers. And, right enough, the big man from Ipswich developed a wee love affair with Scotland.

He fell out with the subject of this book and then they fell in again as he began his globetrotting post-Rangers career, which took him to Coventry and to Sunderland, before he started to play a game of tig with life north of the border. Tel rocked up as assistant to Eric Black at Motherwell and succeeded him shortly afterwards. He even took them to the League Cup final, where they lost heavily to, well, of course, Rangers. There were spells in Australia and at Brentford after that, before he took the road back north again to become assistant to Scotland manager George Burley for the 2010 World Cup campaign. The former captain of England, remember.

But his heart was in the Highlands. He became manager of Inverness Caledonian Thistle and took them to the Premier League. And then he became boss of Hibs. Not bad for a man who had been returned to England by Graeme. He was all over the place after that, including the Philippines and China, but he is still adored by fans of Rangers and the love is mutual.

The fallout is history now. Butcher reflects all these years later that it was a huge compliment that Souness would do whatever was required to get him to Ibrox. 'I had other clubs wanting me,' he said, 'but Souness's admiration of me excited me. In truth, I was a certainty to sign from day one.'

The point is that none of this would have come to pass had Souness not walked into Ibrox those forty years ago. It was him who applied the jump leads to a place that had gone flat. People – like Butcher and Woods and Mo Johnston – had their life paths changed by what he did. He was controlling fate itself.

Despite the money on offer and the fact that English clubs were banned from Europe, I am not sure the English stars would have come north for anyone else. It was Graeme's profile and his status as captain of Europe-conquering Liverpool that swayed it. There was a lot of 'well, if it is good enough for him' thinking going on.

It is four decades. Think on that. As far removed now as Souness at the time was from the immediate post-war Rangers and names like Willie Thornton, Jimmy Duncanson, Jock Shaw and Willie Waddell, Bobby Brown and Sammy Cox. Back then, Bill Struth was in merely his twenty-sixth season as manager. There would be another eight. And he was just the club's second manager. Very different times. As different as 1986 was from what we see now.

It was a year in which the club won the first post-war title and the first-ever League Cup. Forty years on, history would repeat itself. Graeme Souness took a power hose to the cobwebs clinging to Ibrox and shook the place out its slumbers. Rangers were reset. Souness changed the entire direction of the club's policies and attitude to life. He would never have given it a second thought, but he was one very courageous man, considering everything that had gone before.

The first-ever player-manager-director in British football, maybe world football, had a special relationship with his players. He knew Mo Johnston had the character to handle everything that was thrown at him. And he knew how to embrace the staff and make them feel part of it all. He loved Doddie Soutar – the assistant kitman – and frequently pulled him into team pictures when trophies had just been won. But that player-manager role put him in a delicate situation sometimes. Stay with the boys or stand back?

He was good at reading the script. Or maybe at times he wasn't told what was going on.

On one bonding trip – to, I think, St Andrews – things got a little out of hand and the players were ordering and charging top-shelf champagne to their rooms, the bills for which had to be settled in the morning. The big-name players were looking at hundreds of pounds. Curiously, Doddie's was highest of all. Even curiouser, the room shared by McCoist and Durrant was a modest £47. I don't think you need to be Columbo to work that one out. In the end the players squared it all, but I guarantee the manager would have sorted it with that look with the raised eyebrows.

The recipe for Graeme Souness is not freely available, but it would take a Michelin-starred chef to work it all out. He can be scary at times, and it must have been the stuff of nightmares to confront him in midfield when he was in his pomp. He ruled his players with an iron fist and did not particularly care – as Terry Butcher and Graham Roberts will testify – about their reputations or relationships with the support. And yet even those who were sent on their way, Derek Ferguson to Hearts for example, remain full of respect for their former manager. 'My discipline could have been better, but I could see it from his side,' he said. 'I had seven years at the club and he moved me on, but I absolutely loved it. I'll never say a bad word about him.'

And so it goes on. You'll search hard to find a Rangers player of his era who has a bad word to say about Graeme.

If you were not there back in the summer of '86, and then in July three years later when the earth moved and the heavens rumbled as Mo Johnston, a high-profile former Celtic player and a Roman Catholic who was supposed to be re-signing for his boyhood heroes, walked into the Blue Room – then we have tried to make you understand in this book.

It was all very astonishing. Like the invention of the internal combustion engine when suddenly people saw vehicles move without horses. That kind of disbelief.

The bigotry, Scotland's cancer, has not disappeared because of what Graeme Souness did back then. Recent events have proved so. Likewise on the racism front with Mark Walters. But no one cares about the colour or religion of Rangers players any more. And that is just about all football managers can do. Flush away the very concept. Graeme saw the bigger picture, that the club were handicapping themselves as surely as if their players were performing barefooted with their arms tied behind their backs.

Football and religion are no bedfellows. Bloody obvious now, but for a century and more there were people who had no interest in that philosophy. Graeme Souness, in a heartbeat, saw things that generations of custodians of Glasgow Rangers did not and he blew their ideas to smithereens. Or, given the circumstances, Kingdom Come.

But more than that, he steered Rangers – with a lot of assistance from Lawrence Marlborough and David Holmes and then David Murray – down a different road. For a while the club could hardly hand-pick the best players in Scotland, the refusal of Willie Miller to leave Aberdeen for his native city a case in point, but suddenly they were wooing the spine of the England team.

We will never again see the likes of what Souness did because it only needed doing once and he was the first with the cojones to do it. And you know what? Yes, there were people who ripped up their season tickets and some who howled at the moon, but in stark contrast to the beliefs of those who reminisced about the seventeenth century, Ibrox became box-office and the crowds flocked back. He dragged one of the biggest clubs in Britain kicking and screaming into the twentieth century.

The day they signed Mo, television reporters sought vox pops with the old-school dinosaurs who were choking on their pints at the very horror of it all. I dare say there are one or two who never darkened the doorsteps of the stadium ever again. They were clearly in the minority. But there were a few who moved beyond their initial reactions and crawled back.

In his years at the club, Graeme increased turnover and profits season on season, to the stage where you really needed a season ticket to get yourself in the Rangers gang. The average home attendance increased almost every single year.

He still oozes love for Glasgow Rangers. I sensed it through the writing of this book. And mostly he remembered with a smile on his face and a twinkle in his eye. That's the indication of true love.

It was a precious five years of a life that has so far stretched into its seventy-fourth year and been lived in a style that few could ever know. Speak his surname only and no one will confuse him with any other member of his clan.

Messi. Eusébio, Pelé. Cruyff. Best. One word does it. Souness.

And despite the observation that religion should have no part in the game, I'll maybe concede this. Rangers fans should get down on their knees and give prayers of thanks for his coming . . .

Chick Young

Acknowledgements

My heartfelt thanks go to Chick Young, my co-author, for his hard work, friendship and unwavering trust throughout our years working together.

I am deeply grateful to Sir Alex Ferguson for his kind, generous and thoughtful foreword, which opens this book.

I would also like to thank my agent, George Woffenden at Blueprintx, and my publishing agent, Nick Walters at David Luxton Associates, whose guidance and support helped bring this book to life.

My sincere gratitude goes to the outstanding team at Penguin, who have done a remarkable job bringing this account of the most significant period of my professional life into print. In particular, I would like to thank my editor, Shyam Kumar; Joe Cooper in Marketing; Anna Lambert in Publicity; Natalie Wall in Editorial Management; and Annie Underwood in Production.

Finally, I would like to thank the exceptional team at Rangers FC. Their tireless work behind the scenes, along with their championing of the book through to publication, have been invaluable in helping it reach its readers.